The Prague Coup

HARD CASE CRIME
TITAN COMICS

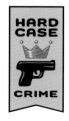

FROM TITAN COMICS AND HARD CASE CRIME

GRAPHIC NOVELS

THE ASSIGNMENT

BABYLON BERLIN

BREAKNECK

MICKEY SPILLANE'S MIKE HAMMER

MILLENNIUM: THE GIRL WITH THE DRAGON TATTOO

MILLENNIUM: THE GIRL WHO PLAYED WITH FIRE

MILLENNIUM: THE GIRL WHO KICKED THE HORNET'S NEST

MILLENNIUM: THE GIRL WHO DANCED WITH DEATH

MINKY WOODCOCK: THE GIRL WHO HANDCUFFED HOUDINI

NORMANDY GOLD

PEEPLAND

THE PRAGUE COUP

QUARRY'S WAR

TRIGGERMAN

TYLER CROSS: BLACK ROCK

TYLER CROSS: ANGOLA

NOVELS

361

A BLOODY BUSINESS

A DIET OF TREACLE

A TOUCH OF DEATH

A WALK AMONG THE TOMBSTONES

BABY MOLL

BINARY

BLACKMAILER

BLOOD ON THE MINK

BORDERLINE

BRAINQUAKE

BRANDED WOMAN

BROTHERS KEEPERS

BUST

CASINO MOON

CHARLESGATE CONFIDENTIAL

CHOKE HOLD

THE COCKTAIL WAITRESS

THE COMEDY IS FINISHED

THE CONFESSION

THE CONSUMMATA

THE CORPSE WORE PASTIES

THE COUNT OF 9

CUT ME IN

THE CUTIE

THE DEAD MAN'S BROTHER

DEAD STREET

DEADLY BELOVED

DRUG OF CHOICE

DUTCH UNCLE

EASY DEATH

EASY GO

FADE TO BLONDE

FAKE I.D.

FALSE NEGATIVE

FIFTY-TO-ONE

FOREVER AND A DEATH

GETTING OFF: A NOVEL OF SEX AND VIOLENCE

THE GIRL WITH THE DEEP BLUE EYES

THE GIRL WITH THE LONG GREEN HEART

GRAVE DESCEND

GRIFTER'S GAME

GUN WORK

THE GUTTER AND THE GRAVE

HELP I AM BEING HELD PRISONER

HOME IS THE SAILOR

HONEY IN HIS MOUTH

HOUSE DICK

JOYLAND

KILL NOW PAY LATER

KILLING CASTRO

THE KNIFE SLIPPED

THE LAST MATCH

THE LAST STAND

LEMONS NEVER LIE

LITTLE GIRL LOST

LOSERS LIVE LONGER

LUCKY AT CARDS

THE MAX

MEMORY

MONEY SHOT

MURDER IS MY BUSINESS

THE NICE GUYS

NIGHT WALKER

NO HOUSE LIMIT

NOBODY'S ANGEL

ODDS ON

PASSPORT TO PERIL

PIMP

PLUNDER OF THE SUN

ROBBIE'S WIFE

SAY IT WITH BULLETS

SCRATCH ONE

THE SECRET LIVES OF MARRIED WOMEN

SEDUCTION OF THE INNOCENT

SINNER MAN

SLIDE

SNATCH

SO MANY DOORS

SO NUDE, SO DEAD

SOHO SINS

SOMEBODY OWES ME MONEY

SONGS OF INNOCENCE

STOP THIS MAN!

STRAIGHT CUT

THIEVES FALL OUT

TOP OF THE HEAP

THE TRIUMPH OF THE SPIDER MONKEY

TURN ON THE HEAT

THE TWENTY-YEAR DEATH

TWO FOR THE MONEY

UNDERSTUDY FOR DEATH

THE VALLEY OF FEAR

THE VENGEFUL VIRGIN

THE VENOM BUSINESS

WEB OF THE CITY

WITNESS TO MYSELF

THE WOUNDED AND THE SLAIN

ZERO COOL

QUARRY

THE FIRST QUARRY

THE LAST QUARRY

QUARRY

QUARRY'S CHOICE

QUARRY'S CLIMAX

QUARRY'S CUT

QUARRY'S DEAL

QUARRY'S EX

QUARRY'S LIST

QUARRY'S VOTE

QUARRY IN THE BLACK

QUARRY IN THE MIDDLE

THE WRONG QUARRY

The *Prague* Coup

WRITER
JEAN-LUC FROMENTAL

ARTIST
MILES HYMAN

TRANSLATOR
LARA VERGNAUD

EDITOR
JONATHAN STEVENSON

TITAN COMICS

Design: Wilfried Tshikana-Ekutshu

Consulting Editor: Charles Ardai

Managing & Launch Editor: Andrew James

Senior Production Controller: Jackie Flook

Production Supervisor: Maria Pearson

Production Controller: Peter James

Production Assistant: Rhiannon Roy

Art Director: Oz Browne

Senior Sales Manager: Steve Tothill

Circulation Executive: Frances Hallam

Press Officer: Will O'Mullane

Direct Sales & Marketing Manager: Ricky Claydon

Brand Manager: Chris Thompson

Publicist: Imogen Harris

Commercial Manager: Michelle Fairlamb

Ads & Marketing Assistant: Bella Hoy

Publishing Manager: Darryl Tothill

Publishing Director: Chris Teather

Operations Director: Leigh Baulch

Executive Director: Vivian Cheung

Publisher: Nick Landau

THE PRAGUE COUP

9781785868870

Published by Titan Comics. A division of Titan Publishing Group Ltd. 144 Southwark St., London, SE1 0UP.
Titan Comics is a registered trademark of Titan Publishing Group, Ltd. All rights reserved.

Originally published in French as Le Coup De Prague © Dupuis 2017. All rights reserved. The name *Hard Case Crime* and the Hard Case Crime logo are trademarks of Winterfall LLC. Hard Case Crime Comics are produced with editorial guidance from Charles Ardai

A CIP catalogue record for this title is available from the British Library

10 9 8 7 6 5 4 3 2 1

First Published December 2018

Printed in China.

Titan Comics.

I'd like to thank

Philippe Garnier (USA)
who gave me *The Enemy Within* by
Michael Shelden, and thus became
this project's sponsor;

Lili Sztajn,
who agreed to have Graham Greene
to dinner (and sometimes even
breakfast) so often and for so long;

José-Louis Bocquet,
a present, precise, and precious
editor, whose angelic patience merits
the highest possible praise;

Carole and Miles Hyman,
beautiful people – it is always
a pleasure and a privilege to work
with you;

Philippe Ghielmetti,
who can make anything more
beautiful;

and all the authors behind the
torrent of words that carried my
work and swept away my certitudes.

JEAN-LUC FROMENTAL

Thank you to

José-Louis Bocquet, a friend and
unrivaled editor, for all his trust in us
since the beginning of this project;

Julie Jonart and the entire Dupuis/
Aire Libre team – thank you for your
support, your patience, and your
immense talent;

Jean-Luc and Lili: this book is
the product of countless years of
precious friendship and of rich and
stimulating collaborations that have
taught me so much – many thanks to
you both!

Finally, I want to thank my wife,
Carole Schilling-Hyman, who was
involved in this project from the
very beginning, strolled down
Vienna's narrow streets with me in
the middle of winter, and above all,
lent her critical eye and honest and
invariably spot-on feedback to make
The Prague Coup the best book
possible.

MILES HYMAN

When it all happened, I was no longer a young girl, but I still had the romanticism and the sense of adventure of the debutante whose bright, preordained future had been hijacked by the War...

Part actress, part spy, when the fighting finally ended, I had placed my talents in the service of London Films, the company owned by Sir Alexander Korda.

Winter 1948. The coldest winter since the War. A Siberian front had buried Vienna under a shroud of ice. Sir Alex had tasked me with welcoming G. upon his arrival from London.

My job was to guide him through the Allied-occupied capital and assist him with his research in writing the film that he, Korda, and Carol Reed were planning to film there.

LONDON FLIGHT JUST GOT IN, MISS!

G. and I had met before at Shepperton Studios. I was a huge fan of his work and was overjoyed by my mission.

But something was bothering me. In a cable sent from Brighton the previous Thursday, G. had warned me of a delay and had asked me to send a telegraph to his wife: "Arrived safely -- kisses -- Graham."

That was all it took to spark a young and romantic girl's imagination...

As I waited on that freezing February night, I wondered what he might have done with his stolen weekend.

SORRY TO HAVE MADE YOU BRAVE THIS BLIZZARD, MISS MONTAGU!

MR. GREENE?

YOU TOLD THE PRESS I WAS COMING?

NOT AT ALL, SIR!

FAST, FOR A FOUR-EYES. DO YOU KNOW HIM?

NO. VIENNA'S A REVOLVING DOOR, YOU KNOW...

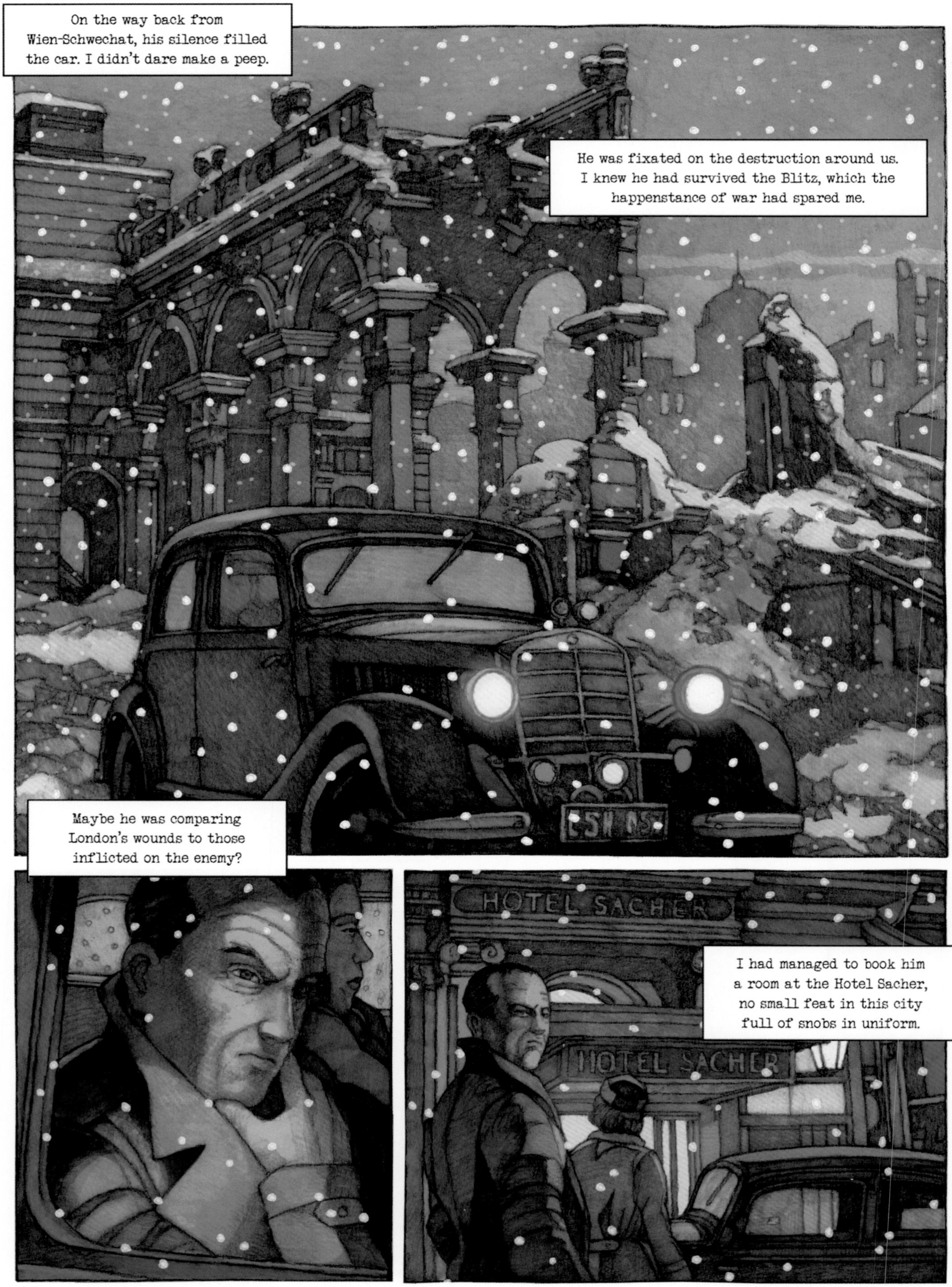
On the way back from Wien-Schwechat, his silence filled the car. I didn't dare make a peep.
He was fixated on the destruction around us. I knew he had survived the Blitz, which the happenstance of war had spared me.
Maybe he was comparing London's wounds to those inflicted on the enemy?
HOTEL SACHER
I had managed to book him a room at the Hotel Sacher, no small feat in this city full of snobs in uniform.
HOTEL SACHER

IS THE ROOM TO YOUR LIKING, SIR?

GRAHAM, ENSIGN MONTAGU! WE'RE TO BE STATIONED TOGETHER, IF I UNDERSTOOD CORRECTLY.

His reference to my rank moved me deeply. He had taken it upon himself to inquire about my military past.

IS THE ROOM TO YOUR LIKING, GRAHAM?

IT'S A BIT CHILLY, BUT I HAVE JUST THE THING...

...THE PILGRIM'S FRIEND!

We drank, forgetting about the officials waiting for him at Blaue Bar.

WHAT'S HE DOING IN VIENNA, COLONEL? SINCE YOU'RE IN THE KNOW...

CINEMA, I HEAR. LONDON FILMS IS MAKING A FILM HERE.

WITH A LITTLE LUCK, MISS VIVIEN LEIGH WILL BE JAZZING UP OUR EVENINGS IN NO TIME.

HAVE YOU READ HIS BOOKS?

CONFIDENTIAL AGENT, ORIENT EXPRESS, A GUN FOR SALE. GOOD THRILLERS, ACTUALLY.

WHAT HE CALLS HIS DIVERSIONS. BUT HIS SERIOUS NOVELS ARE MOST PRAISEWORTHY. *THE MAN WITHIN*, *THE POWER AND THE GLORY*, AND HIS LATEST, *THE HEART OF THE MATTER*, WHICH IS SUPPOSED TO BE EXCELLENT...

THERE'S NO DOUBT HE'S OUR BEST CATHOLIC AUTHOR, MUCH BETTER THAN MAURIAC OR BERNANOS, IF YOU ASK ME.

I ONLY READ WESTERNS.

GRAHAM, THIS IS COLONEL BEAUCLERK, FROM THE INFORMATION SERVICE OF THE ALLIED COMMISSION. HE'LL BE A GREAT HELP TO US IN OUR RESEARCH.

AND OF COURSE MAJOR MILLIGAN HERE KNOWS VIENNA INSIDE AND OUT, RIGHT, MAJOR?

A DECEPTIVE CITY, SIR. YOU HAVE TO BE ON YOUR TOES.

DUDDLEY GRABBIT, BRITISH COUNCIL. IF I MAY, SIR. HOW CAN A WRITER OF YOUR STATURE APPLY HIS GENIUS TO SOMETHING AS TRIVIAL AS CINEMA?

MONEY, MR...

...GRABBIT. I WAS HOPING TO CONVINCE YOU TO COME SPEAK AT OUR BOOK CLUB. THE CITY OF MOZART IS DYING FROM A LACK OF CULTURE...

AND A FEW TENS OF THOUSANDS OF TONS OF OUR BOMBS, RIGHT, MR. GRABBIT?

KEEP THEM KOMMEN, MEYER!

If there was one thing that could rival the quantity of explosives dropped on Vienna...

...it was our consumption of alcohol

The next day, in surprisingly good form after the night's libations, he wanted to visit a cemetery. I took him to Zentralfriedhof, the resting place of Beethoven and Salieri...

MOZART'S TOMB IS EMPTY.

WHEN HE DIED, THEY BURIED HIM IN SECRET IN THE OLD ST. MARX CEMETERY DURING A WINTER JUST AS COLD AS THIS ONE...

BUT WHEN THEY WANTED TO BRING HIM HERE, TO GIVE HIM A BURIAL PLACE WORTHY OF HIS NAME, THEY COULDN'T FIND THE BODY.

Clearly, G. attracted photographers.
This one was an old acquaintance.
A ghost from a secret period of my life.

I recognized his team, too. Bud Boots and his Merry Men, tasked with my protection five years earlier in Zurich, when I was helping the Americans by debriefing a German vice consul involved in a plot against Hitler...

What were they doing in Vienna?

Allen Dulles, our chief, had returned to the U.S. where he was trying to transform the old OSS into a spanking new CIA.

HOW ODD...

WHAT?

THE SCRIPT THAT I SOLD TO KORDA OPENS WITH THE STORY OF AN EMPTY GRAVE, LIKE MOZART'S...

I HAD PAID MY LAST FAREWELL TO HARRY A WEEK AGO, WHEN HIS COFFIN WAS LOWERED INTO THE FROZEN FEBRUARY GROUND, SO IT WAS WITH INCREDULITY THAT I SAW HIM PASS BY AMONG THE HOST OF STRANGERS IN THE STRAND.

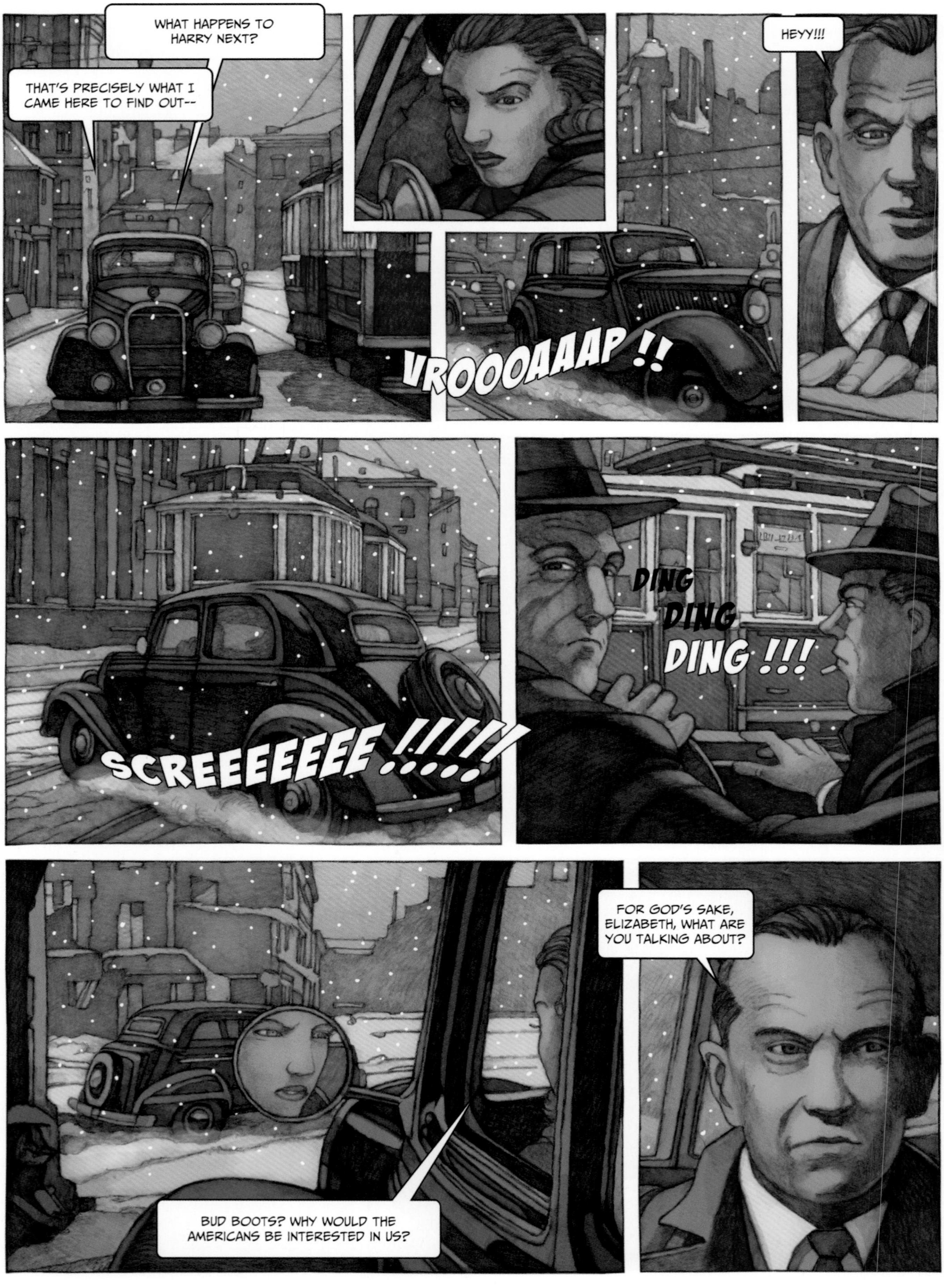
WHAT HAPPENS TO HARRY NEXT?
THAT'S PRECISELY WHAT I CAME HERE TO FIND OUT--
HEYY!!!
VROOOAAAP !!
SCREEEEEEEE !!!!!!
DING DING DING !!!
BUD BOOTS? WHY WOULD THE AMERICANS BE INTERESTED IN US?
FOR GOD'S SAKE, ELIZABETH, WHAT ARE YOU TALKING ABOUT?

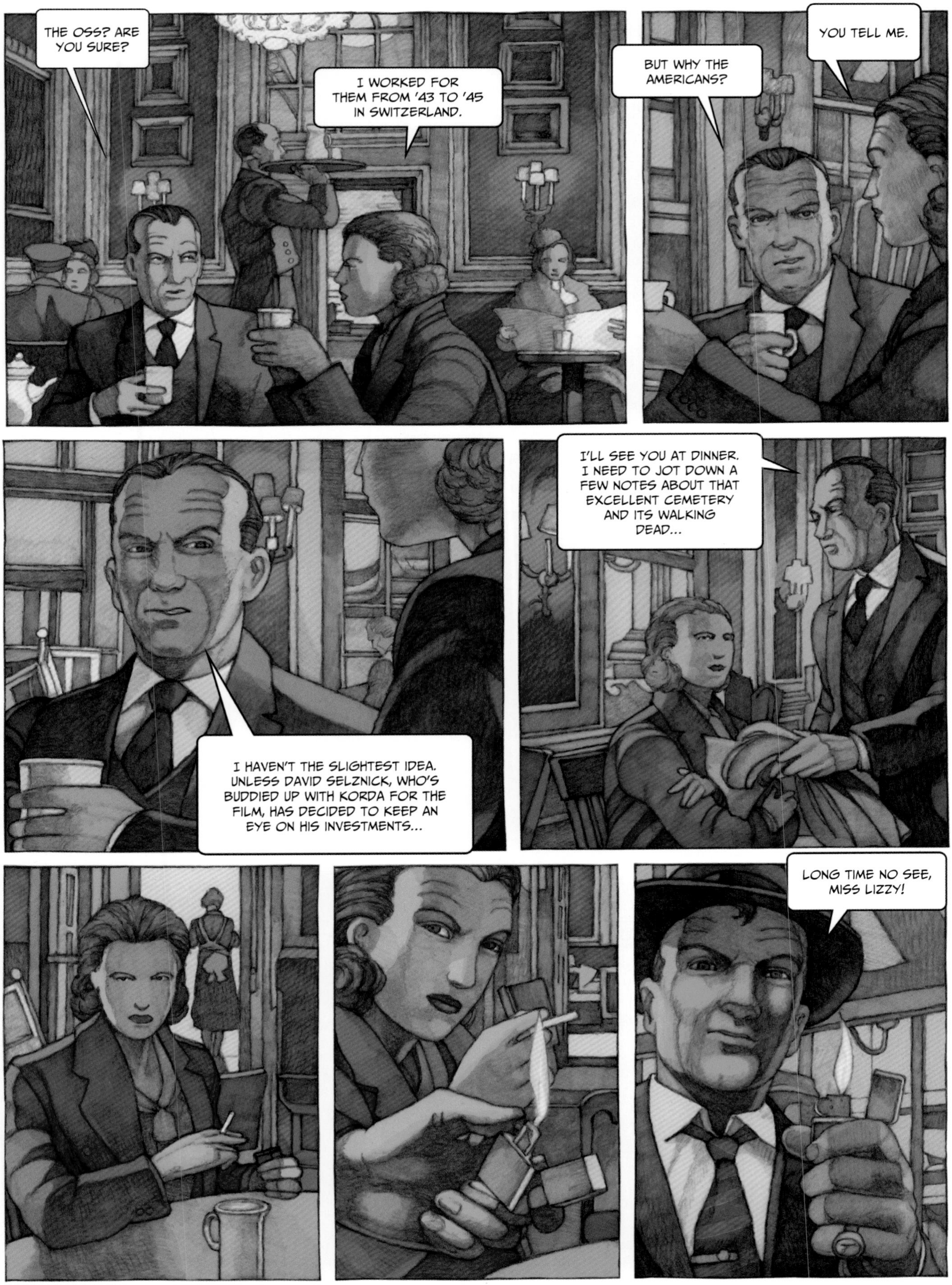
THE OSS? ARE YOU SURE?
I WORKED FOR THEM FROM '43 TO '45 IN SWITZERLAND.
BUT WHY THE AMERICANS?
YOU TELL ME.
I HAVEN'T THE SLIGHTEST IDEA. UNLESS DAVID SELZNICK, WHO'S BUDDIED UP WITH KORDA FOR THE FILM, HAS DECIDED TO KEEP AN EYE ON HIS INVESTMENTS...
I'LL SEE YOU AT DINNER. I NEED TO JOT DOWN A FEW NOTES ABOUT THAT EXCELLENT CEMETERY AND ITS WALKING DEAD...
LONG TIME NO SEE, MISS LIZZY!

BUD BOOTS! WHAT ARE YOU DOING IN VIENNA?

I ASSUME YOU'RE FAMILIAR WITH THE TERM "COLD WAR"?

TWO SUPERPOWERS DIVVIED UP THE WORLD AND NOW THEY'RE EACH RESTRAINING THEMSELVES FROM ATTACKING THE OTHER SO THEY CAN DOMINATE IT?

NICELY PUT. LET'S JUST SAY THAT I'M ONE OF THE ESKIMOS CHARGED WITH MAKING SURE THE TEMPERATURE DOESN'T GO UP. DO YOU KNOW WHY YOUR BIG SHOT'S HERE?

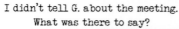

FOR A FILM.

ARE YOU SURE THAT'S THE ONLY REASON HE CAME TO VIENNA?

Boots asked me if I was willing to keep an eye out like back in the day. When I asked where his orders came from, he pointed to the ceiling of the Sacher café. I doubt he meant it literally.

I didn't tell G. about the meeting. What was there to say?

I SPOKE TO LONDON ABOUT YOUR WILLIAM "BUD" BOOTS, A FORMER SPY AND NOW A REPORTER FOR LIFE.

WHICH WOULD EXPLAIN HIS INTEREST IN ME, GIVEN HOW HIS BOSS, HENRY LUCE, IS OBSESSED WITH ME.

I refrained from commenting that Life reporters are rarely escorted by hulking bodyguards like Leroy and Jones.

At dinner, he asked me about my work for the OSS and sarcastically described his own activities as a spy during the War.

WHEN I WAS POSTED IN FREETOWN, I SUGGESTED CREATING A TRAVELING BROTHEL TO GLEAN INFORMATION FROM OFFICIALS OF THE VICHY REGIME.

NO ONE AGREED...

WE SPENT AS MUCH TIME MAKING UP STORIES TO THE ENEMY'S BENEFIT AS WE DID RIFLING THROUGH ITS DIRTY LAUNDRY. IN SHORT, THE WRITER'S DAILY GRIND...

THEN I JOINED MI6 IN LONDON, ID NUMBER 59200, SECTION V, A GOOD OL' BOYS CLUB THAT REVOLVED AROUND DRINKING AND PLAYING AT WAR.

MR. GREENE? BARON GEORG VON KURTZ.

SO SORRY TO INTERRUPT THIS CHARMING TÊTE-À-TÊTE. I HAD PLANNED TO PAY YOU A VISIT AT THE SACHER, BUT SINCE OUR PATHS FORTUITOUSLY CROSSED HERE...

The Baron wasn't really sorry. A second later, he requested a chair, to the great pleasure of G., who was delighted to welcome a vestige of old vienna to his table.

Von Kurtz suggested they continue the evening elsewhere. I dropped them off at the Casanova and made up a migraine so I wouldn't have to stay.

I had better things to do than sit around looking at sad, malnourished bodies.

AH, MY DEAR! IF YOU COULD CONVINCE THE GREAT MR. GREENE TO ACCEPT MY INVITATION--

NOT TONIGHT, MR. GRABBIT! MY HEAD'S POUNDING.

I wasn't a hotel thief, but I knew how to make friends.

OH, KLAUS, I LEFT SOME NOTES I NEED TO TYPE UP IN THE GENTLEMAN'S ROOM.

YOU'RE AN ANGEL, KLAUS!

I hadn't even started digging when my transgression paid off. The woman in the photo wasn't G.'s wife. I had my explanation for the stolen weekend.

Rumors of his infidelity had been rampant in London, but this time the affair seemed serious...

CAFRYN MY LOVE,

YOUR PHOTO HAS A PLACE OF HONOR UNDER MY LAMP, AND I LOOK AT IT LIKE A SCHOOLBOY IN LOVE FOR THE FIRST TIME. HAVE I EVER FELT THIS WAY BEFORE? THOSE FEW DAYS IN PARADISE HAVE LEFT ME LONGING

Embarrassed by my indecent curiosity, I got back to the reason for my visit: to see if there was any truth to Bud Boots' allegations.

The first notebook contained notes for the film. I was about to open the second one when--

CRACK!

I hit the lights and dove behind the curtains.

If he was one of Boots' men, I'd never seen him before.

He took his time, as if he wasn't worried about being caught.

When the light hit his face, I recognized the photographer from the airport.

He left after conducting an exhaustive search. He clearly hadn't found what he was looking for.

That's when I realized that I was still holding the second notebook.

HARPO

Harpo?

That unusual name was on my mind the next few days as we faithfully followed the itinerary that I had prepared for G.

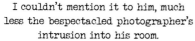

I couldn't mention it to him, much less the bespectacled photographer's intrusion into his room.

...THE ONLY QUESTION IS— HOW MUCH LONGER BEFORE THE NEXT WAR...

BLACK MARKET... SAME OLD...

But the shadowy dance around my author was starting to worry me.

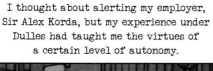

I thought about alerting my employer, Sir Alex Korda, but my experience under Dulles had taught me the virtues of a certain level of autonomy.

I decided to wait and see.

As the days and meetings went by,
I felt G.'s excitement growing.

IT'S TAKING
SHAPE, ELIZABETH!
YOU'RE MY GUARDIAN
ANGEL!

As for me, the feeling of constantly
being watched had me on tenterhooks.

ATELIER SIEVERING

The affable Karl Hartl ran Wien-Film,
partners with London Films.

DON'T HESITATE TO
THINK BIG, MY FRIEND!

He had held the post throughout the War
without getting too mixed up with the Nazis.

SIR ALEX TOLD ME THAT HE WON'T
SKIMP ON THE BUDGET. LONDON
CAPITAL THAT'S BEEN BLOCKED
SINCE THE WAR AND CAN ONLY
BE SPENT IN AUSTRIA...

I HOPE THAT YOUR STAY IN OUR BATTERED VIENNA HAS PAID OFF.

BEYOND MY EXPECTATIONS, HERR HARTL.

OH, I RECEIVED DOCUMENTS FROM LONDON THAT YOU NEED TO SIGN...

RUN ALONG, ELIZABETH, I'LL MEET YOU AT THE SACHER.

Being so rudely dismissed didn't exactly improve my mood. What could Hartl have to say to G. that I couldn't hear?

HAVE WE LOST OUR PROTÉGÉ?

FOLLOWING ME, BOOTS?

LOOKING OUT FOR YOU. LET'S WALK.

HAVE YOU THOUGHT ABOUT OUR REQUEST?

IF THERE ARE THINGS TO KNOW ABOUT G., IT'S UP TO YOU TO TELL ME.

I DON'T GET IT, BUD. WHAT COULD I TELL YOU THAT YOU DON'T ALREADY KNOW?

YOU'RE MONITORING ALL OF OUR COMINGS AND GOINGS.

I didn't tell him about the photographer's visit to G.'s room. When I asked again about the supposed "other reasons" for his presence in Vienna...

...I got a startling reply.

THERE'S A POSSIBILITY THAT HE'S WORKING FOR HIS OLD BOSSES AGAIN.

Meaning the Intelligence Service.

I found G. at Blaue Bar, where he was getting a head start on the day's drinking schedule.

WHERE'D YOU GO, MY DEAR? I GOT BACK WELL BEFORE YOU.

I had to talk to him. But about what exactly? And how?

THAT HARTL IS THE MODEL OF AN OBLIGING AUSTRIAN.

I couldn't exactly say, "The CIA thinks that you're here on an espionage mission!"

HE GAVE ME A CONTACT WHO COULD BE USEFUL. "THE EYE OF UNDERGROUND VIENNA," HE SAID.

A CZECH, A REPORTER FOR THE TIMES...

PETER SMOLKA. HE'S ON MY LIST, GRAHAM. WE'RE SEEING HIM TOMORROW.

I FORGOT THAT YOU'RE MY GODSEND, ENSIGN MONTAGU.

FOR YOUR TROUBLE, LET ME TAKE YOU OUT TONIGHT. A FASCINATING SPOT THAT, WITH A LITTLE LUCK, YOU'VE NEVER BEEN TO BEFORE.

I don't know if never having been to The Oriental was a matter of luck...

SLIVOVITZ!

...but I quickly learned where G. had heard about it.

True baron or not, von Kurtz clearly made his living by bringing clients to such establishments.

HE'LL JOIN US "AS SOON AS INGE FINISHES HER ACT."

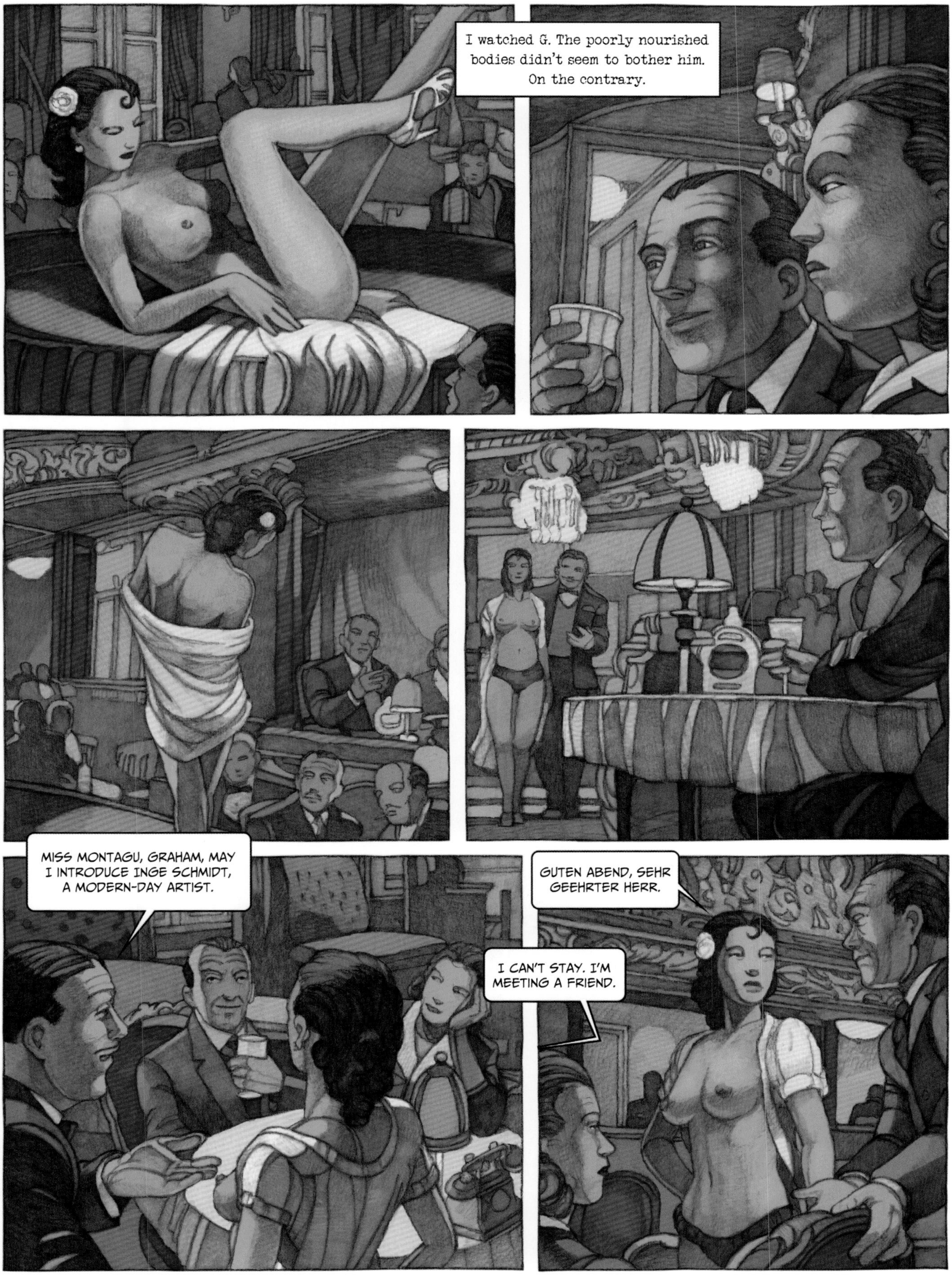
I watched G. The poorly nourished bodies didn't seem to bother him. On the contrary.
MISS MONTAGU, GRAHAM, MAY I INTRODUCE INGE SCHMIDT, A MODERN-DAY ARTIST.
GUTEN ABEND, SEHR GEEHRTER HERR.
I CAN'T STAY. I'M MEETING A FRIEND.

I didn't like the turn the evening was taking.

I'LL BE RIGHT BACK.

I recognized von Kurtz's "friend."

When I came back, our modern-day artist was gone...

INGE LEFT ALREADY?

WE LACKED A COMMON LANGUAGE.

HUNGER WITH NO APPETITE IS THE DEVIL'S TORMENT...

GRAHAM, YOU SHOULD BE CAREFUL WITH VON KURTZ.

HE'S A HARMLESS ENOUGH PIMP. AND HE PLAYS THE TRAITOR SPLENDIDLY...

I JUST SAW HIM WITH THAT AIRPORT PHOTOGRAPHER.

I BET THAT OLD REVELER KNOWS ALL THE DREGS OF VIENNA.

OH, INGE... INGE...

Alcohol and annoyance made me bold.

TELL ME, GRAHAM... HOW DOES YOUR CATHOLIC FAITH TOLERATE THIS KIND OF PLACE AND PEOPLE?

A FRIEND WHO WAS OFTEN ASKED THAT QUESTION HAD THE HABIT OF RESPONDING...

..."YOU CAN'T IMAGINE WHO I WOULD BE WITHOUT RELIGION. WITHOUT DIVINE ASSISTANCE, I WOULD BARELY DESERVE TO BE CALLED HUMAN."

THE POLISH BRANDY GOT THE BEST OF ME. IF YOU GO OUT, CAN YOU POST THIS FOR ME?

OF COURSE.

AND WHAT TIME IS THE MEETING WITH THE CZECH?

THIS EVENING.

OFF FOR SOME ASPIRIN AND HOT LEMON.

I had no doubt that he was testing me. That was typical of him.

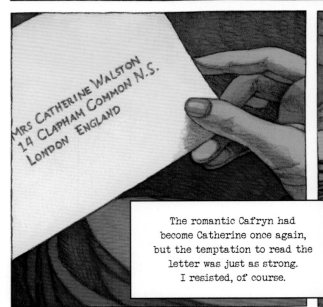

MRS CATHERINE WALSTON
14 CLAPHAM COMMON N.S.
LONDON ENGLAND

The romantic Cafryn had become Catherine once again, but the temptation to read the letter was just as strong. I resisted, of course.

George Orwell included Peter Smolka in the list of suspected Communist sympathizers that he created shortly before his death.

But at the time, he just seemed like an excellent reporter, and an expert in Vienna's black markets.

EVENING, MISS MONTAGU, WELCOME MR. GREENE!

THERE'S TEA IN THE SAMOVAR, IF YOU WANT TO WARM YOURSELVES UP.

HOW CAN I BE OF SERVICE, MY GOOD MAN?

I'M LOOKING FOR A CRIMINAL ACTIVITY FOR MY PROTAGONIST HARRY. RARE ENOUGH NOT TO MAKE HIM A COMMON CRIMINAL, SERIOUS ENOUGH THAT HE'LL NEED TO DISAPPEAR.

WELL, THERE IS NO SHORTAGE OF POSSIBILITIES.

IN TERMS OF CRIME, VIENNA HAS EVERYTHING YOU NEED.

ELIZABETH... I BROUGHT A BOTTLE OF SCOTCH FOR OUR FRIEND, WHICH I LEFT IN THE CAR. IF YOU WOULDN'T MIND...

He was sidelining me again. But this time...

...I had no intention...

...of being pushed around so easily.

IF I UNDERSTAND CORRECTLY, YOU'RE CHASING A GHOST, MR. GREENE.

OF CHRISTMAS PAST, LET'S JUST SAY.

By the time I got back, Harry had become Harpo.

BUT WHAT COULD I TELL YOU ABOUT HARPO THAT YOU DON'T ALREADY KNOW?

YOU WERE HERE DURING HIS STAY IN '34, ISN'T THAT RIGHT? I WAS TOLD YOU'RE THE ONE WHO INTRODUCED HIM TO LITZI.

CORRECT, BUT I DON'T SEE--

MEEOW !

ELIZABETH?

FOUND THE BOTTLE.

When we left Smolka, well past midnight, the scotch had been polished off and Harpo hadn't been mentioned again.

THAT CHAP WAS A GOLD MINE. THANKS, ANGEL.

THANK HARTL, THE OBLIGING AUSTRIAN!

CRRRRRRRRR

FAHREN SIE HIN!

WHAT'S WRONG?

PROBLEM, FRÄULEIN?

RUN, GRAHAM!

CLACK
CLACK
CLACK
CLACK!

VROOOOOOOOOOOO

KEEP THIS SAFE FOR ME. IT'S VERY IMPORTANT.

NO, GRAHAM... WAIT!

EVERYTHING OKAY, MISS MONTAGU?

MAJOR MILLIGAN! THANK GOODNESS!

KEINE BEWEGUNG, HERR GREENE!

WEEEEEOOOOOO

The heaven-sent major brought us back to our car...

TWO INDIVIDUALS! THEY DISAPPEARED!

WHAT DID THEY WANT?

I HAVE NO IDEA, MAJOR.

THE GAS PIPE'S BEEN CUT CLEAN, SIR!

Bud Boots, von Kurtz, Hartl, Smolka, Harpo, Litzi...

Karl Hartl had directed G. to Smolka, and the baron's "friends" had been waiting outside Smolka's home.

The names danced around in my foggy mind like the pieces of a mysterious chess game.

Yet, Hartl was Korda's man, and rumor had it that Sir Alex had placed his fortune and networks at the disposal of the Intelligence Service.

If my employer had charged G. with a risky mission, he hadn't thought fit to inform me.

The first one very realistically described trafficking in adulterated penicillin and its ravages on the population of Vienna.

The "very important" folder that G. had entrusted to me contained texts mixing fiction and reportage, clearly written by Smolka.

A LARGE SCALE BLACK-MARKET IN PENICILLIN, MORE THAN OFTEN PAST ITS USED-BY DATE OR DANGEROUSLY DILUTED, CONTROLLED BY GANGS USING THE SEWERS AS A HIDEOUT

Another described the highly complex sewer system that stretched out under the city.

The third was about the workers' revolution of February '34, crushed by Dollfuss's fascist regime. Maybe this one had to do with Harpo, but--

KNOCK KNOCK....

I HOPE THAT I DIDN'T WAKE YOU. I'M HERE TO GET SMOLKA'S PAPERS BACK.

DON'T YOU THINK THAT YOU HAD BETTER TELL ME EVERYTHING?

TELL YOU WHAT, MY DEAR? I DON'T UNDERSTAND TONIGHT'S EVENTS ANY MORE THAN YOU DO.

WHO'S HARPO, FOR EXAMPLE?

He didn't even look surprised.

THE MOST POETIC OF THE MARX BROTHERS, MY FAVORITE. APART FROM KARL, NATURALLY.

I had slept badly, nagged by questions, and he was the last person I wanted to see at breakfast.

He was in bad shape.

BARON? I DIDN'T KNOW YOU WERE AN EARLY BIRD.

IS OUR FRIEND HERE?

HE'S WORKING.

THAT'S UNFORTUNATE. I HAVE A MESSAGE OF THE UTMOST IMPORTANCE FOR HIM.

I CAN PASS IT ON TO HIM, IF YOU LIKE...

YES, LET'S DO THAT. TELL HIM: "HOHER MARKT, MIDNIGHT." HE'LL UNDERSTAND.

YOU KEEP CURIOUS COMPANY, MISS MONTAGU!

DO YOU KNOW THE BARON VON KURTZ?

WE FIND HIM AND SOME OF HIS PEERS BEHIND EVERY GARBAGE CAN IN VIENNA. THE AUSTRO-HUNGARIAN NOBILITY ISN'T WHAT IT USED TO BE.

NEWS ABOUT OUR ATTACKERS, MAJOR?

WE NOW KNOW HOW THEY VANISHED INTO THIN AIR.

IN THE SEWERS?

VIENNA HAS A SPRAWLING GRID. CRIMINALS USE IT TO CIRCULATE BETWEEN ZONES.

CAN YOU ARRANGE A VISIT FOR ME?

TONIGHT, IF YOU LIKE.

I waited for Milligan to leave before telling G. about von Kurtz's visit.

IF IT'S SEWERS YOU WANT, YOU'VE GOT THEM IN SPADES.

The major picked us up at 17:00.

He had done a good job. Special sewer policemen were there to escort us.

VORSICHT STUFE, FRÄULEIN!

1,500 MILES OF TUNNELS... BEGUN UNDER THE ROMANS... HIT 1,800 TIMES BY ALLIED BOMBS...

STOWAWAYS AND THIEVES HAVE BEEN USING THEM FOREVER TO MOVE AROUND UNDER THE CITY...

I sensed a childish excitement overtaking G...

...more due to the place itself than to the major's statistics.

GRAHAM?

TELL ME, ELIZABETH...

AH!

...AFTER THE HORRORS THE WORLD HAS JUST EXPERIENCED, IF THE CREATOR WANTED TO ESCAPE JUDGMENT BY HIS CREATURES, WHERE WOULD HE HIDE, IN YOUR OPINION?

THE ALMIGHTY IN THE SEWERS OF VIENNA? WHAT AN ODD IDEA!

THOUGH THEY AREN'T AS INHOSPITABLE AS I HAD IMAGINED.

DON'T TURN AROUND RIGHT AWAY, MISS.

OH MY GOD!

After the sewers, Hoher Markt looked jovial to me. We were slightly early for our meeting with the baron.

The normal Viennese square was rendered dramatic by the rubble and the light of a little café open late.

Von Kurtz was late. Or he wasn't coming.

THERE HE IS!

WHAT...!!!

SCREEEEEEEEEEE !!!!!!!

He had died instantly.

G. was distraught.

COME ON! WE CAN'T STAY HERE.

TOO LATE!

YOUR NIGHTS ARE CLEARLY MORE EXCITING THAN MY DAYS!

Milligan brought us back to the military police HQ.

Colonel Beauclerk was waiting for us, less friendly than he had been at our first meeting.

IT WOULD APPEAR THAT YOU'RE A MAGNET FOR UNFORTUNATE EVENTS.

JUST ANOTHER TRAFFIC ACCIDENT. YOU MUST HAVE A DOZEN OR SO EVERY NIGHT IN SUCH A BADLY LIT CITY...

VON KURTZ ISN'T JUST ANY OLD PEDESTRIAN.

WE HAVE A LARGE FILE ON HIM. AS FOR YOU...

...YOU WEREN'T THERE BY CHANCE EITHER. THE MAJOR TOLD ME HE SAW YOU DEEP IN CONVERSATION WITH THE BARON THIS MORNING, MISS MONTAGU?

I...

THE BARON HAD AGREED TO GIVE ME INFORMATION ABOUT VIENNA'S BLACK MARKETS, ADULTERATED MEDICATIONS IN PARTICULAR...

The ease with which he lied left me speechless.

VIENNA IS A DANGEROUS PLACE, MY FRIEND. YOU'RE GETTING IN OVER YOUR HEAD.

I WOULDN'T WANT YOUR FILM TO TURN INTO A BAD DETECTIVE MELODRAMA.

I DO HAVE SOME EXPERIENCE IN THAT FIELD.

VON KURTZ WASN'T JUST A SMALL-TIME CROOK INVOLVED IN ALL MANNER OF SLEAZY TRAFFICKING, INCLUDING WHITE SLAVES...

...YOUR BARON ALSO GOT ON VERY WELL WITH THE REICH'S ELITE DURING THE ANSCHLUSS.

THAT'S WHY WE WERE KEEPING AN EYE ON HIM.

HERE HE IS IN DELIGHTFUL COMPANY: GÖRING, HIMMLER, THE GAULEITER JOSEF BÜRCKEL, THE WAR CRIMINAL SEYSS-INQUART...

G. suggested a nightcap at The Oriental. I said that I had had my fill of horrors for the evening.

The Blaue Bar was closing, but the gentleman was resourceful as always.

SCOTCH IN MY ROOM?

I found him both baffling and disconcerting.

The seductive Cafryn gazing at us surely had something to do with it.

NOW THAT A MAN HAS DIED, ARE YOU GOING TO TELL ME THE TRUTH, GRAHAM?

THE TRUTH HAS DONE LESS FOR THE HUMAN RACE THAN SWEET LIES, MY DEAR.

SHADOWS HAVE BEEN CIRCLING US SINCE YOU ARRIVED, AND I DON'T THINK IT'S JUST BECAUSE OF THE FILM.

WHY THEN?

I THINK THAT YOU'RE HERE ON A SPYING MISSION.

WITHIN EVERY WRITER THERE LIES A SPY IN SLUMBER.

WELL WAKE HIM UP! WE'VE HAD TWO BRUSHES WITH DEATH IN TWENTY-FOUR HOURS!

PERHAPS THE HUSBAND OF THAT BEAUTIFUL WOMAN IS TRYING TO TAKE ME OUT. DID YOU THINK OF THAT?

NOW YOU'RE MAKING FUN OF ME.

I'M MOST CERTAINLY NOT, ELIZABETH. BUT IT'S LATE AND DESPITE HOW YOU MAKE ME FEEL, I'M NOT FREE TO FOLLOW MY DESIRES.

Dismissed, yet again.

BOOTS? HOW DID YOU GET IN HERE?

THE SAME WAY I TAUGHT YOU, MISS LIZZY.

I'M AFRAID THIS ISN'T A GOOD TIME. I'VE HAD AN EXHAUSTING DAY.

YES, THINGS ARE HEATING UP!

THAT OLD DEGENERATE GOT HIMSELF SMOKED LIKE A DEER IN THE HEADLIGHTS.

YOU ALREADY KNOW?

WE WERE THERE.

THE DRIVER IS A GUY NAMED RABE. A KILLER WORKING FOR THE RUSSIANS.

MY GOD, HE'S TERRIFYING.

I'M HERE.

Danger rekindles old romances.

Our years together during
the War made any false modesty
or foreplay unnecessary.

DID YOU MEET
INGE, THE BARON'S
PROTÉGÉE?

YES, IN THAT AWFUL
NIGHTCLUB.

QUITE
THE GAL,
HUH?

JUST ANOTHER GIRL FORCED TO
PRANCE AROUND NAKED SO SHE
CAN EAT. THAT'S ALL THERE IS
IN THIS TOWN.

DOES SHE
INTEREST YOUR
WRITER?

SHE CATERS TO HIS
PERVERSE LEANINGS. WHY
DO YOU ASK, BUD?

MY GUYS LOCATED HER.
SHE'S STAYING IN THE
RUSSIAN ZONE. SHE'S
ON THIN ICE, APPARENTLY.

HOW ABOUT
YOU SPELL OUT
WHAT IT IS YOU
WANT FROM
ME?

We were in Vienna. He answered my question with a question.

WHAT DO YOU KNOW ABOUT YOUR AUTHOR?

WHAT EVERYONE KNOWS... AND A FEW THINGS THAT NOBODY KNOWS.

DO YOU KNOW ABOUT HIS SERVICE RECORD IN INTELLIGENCE?

JUST WHAT HE TOLD ME. THE FREETOWN BROTHEL, MI6 IN LONDON...

ESPIONAGE RUNS IN THE GREENE FAMILY.

HIS SISTER, WHO WAS RECRUITED IN '38, IS THE ONE WHO CONVINCED HIM TO JOIN THE INTELLIGENCE SERVICE.

IN '41, HE JOINED SECTION V, IN CHARGE OF THE MADRID, LISBON, GIBRALTAR, AND TANGIER STATIONS, MANAGED BY ANOTHER PUBLIC SCHOOL PRODUCT, KIM PHILBY...

THE GOOD 'OL BOYS CLUB...

DRINKERS, PLAYERS, BULLSHITTERS... THEIR SERVICE HANDLED THE FAMOUS GARBO -- THE AGENT WHO INFILTRATED THE NAZIS AND INVENTED A NETWORK OF 27 BRITISH MOLES, ALL IMAGINARY...

PERFECT STUFF TO IGNITE OUR FRIEND'S MISCHIEVOUS MIND... HE MAY BE AN EXCELLENT NOVELIST, BUT WHEN IT COMES TO ESPIONAGE, HE'S AN AMATEUR...

...AND AN AMATEUR IN OUR FIELD IS LIKE A LOOSE CANNON ON THE DECK OF A SHIP. YOU HAVE NO IDEA HOW MUCH DAMAGE IT CAN CAUSE.

The next day, the snow began to fall again.

The weather made it harder to drive... and shadow.

KNOW WHERE YOU'RE GOING?

THE RUSSIAN ZONE. YOU HAVEN'T FORGOTTEN YOUR ID CARD, HAVE YOU?

ВХОД В СОВЕТСКУЮ ЗОНУ
RUSSISCHE ZONE

HOW DID YOU FIND HER ADDRESS?

I HAVE MY LITTLE SECRETS TOO.

FRAÜLEIN SCHMIDT, BITTE.

NOCH EINMAL? IM DRITTEN STOCK!

THIRD FLOOR. BUT WHY DID SHE SAY "AGAIN"?

JAWOHL?

IS INGE SCHMIDT HERE?

NO. NOT COME HOME LAST NIGHT. I ALREADY TOLD THE OTHER MAN.

WHAT OTHER MAN?

THE ONE WITH THE SCARY MOUTH WHO CAME THIS MORNING. WHAT YOU WANT WITH HER?

TO TALK TO HER. IT'S VERY IMPORTANT. SHE CAN REACH ME HERE.

G. was lunching with the young Austro-Italian actress being offered the leading female role.

One on one, as was fitting.

I left him at Café Mozart before returning to the Sacher to warm up.

When he reappeared after dark, inebriated and satisfied, I almost asked if he had felt "free to follow his desires."

But I had better ways to surprise him than with silly questions...

INGE'S ROOMMATE LEFT THIS FOR YOU.

"INGE WILL SEE YOU TONIGHT AT THE OPERA. RENT A BOX AND WAIT FOR SOMEONE TO CONTACT YOU."

GOOD GOD, ELIZABETH, WHAT TIME IS IT?

YOUR LIFESAVER IS ON TOP OF IT.

With the Wiener Staatsoper damaged by Allied bombs, the opera and operetta, Viennese specialties, had retreated to the venerable Theater an der Wien.

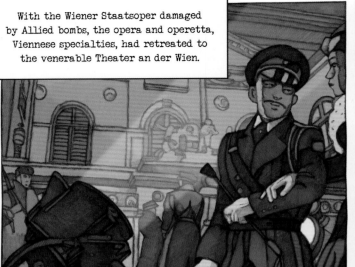

FIDELIO WAS CREATED HERE IN 1805, WITH MIXED REVIEWS.

DEAR ELIZABETH, WHAT A PLEASANT SURPRISE...

WILLIAM BOOTS, *LIFE MAGAZINE*. I WAS HOPING TO MEET YOU, BUT IT'S BEEN HECTIC SINCE I ARRIVED IN VIENNA.

QUITE THE BUSY LITTLE CITY.

I'M HERE FOR A SERIES OF ARTICLES ON "THE NEXT FRONT LINE," AS OUR REVERED DIRECTOR SAYS. I'D LIKE TO HEAR YOUR OPINION ON THE RISK OF THIS COLD WAR HEATING UP.

RIIIIING

ANOTHER TIME PERHAPS. TONIGHT, IT'S BEETHOVEN.

JETZT, SCHÄTZCHEN, JETZT SIND WIR ALLEIN...

SO HAB' ICH DENN NIMMERMEHR RUH...

Was it the magic of Ludwig van? I felt a surge of excitement that I had stopped hoping to feel ever again.

First Bud Boots, then the bespectacled photographer... The only shadow missing was the horrible harelip.

YOUR PROGRAM, MEIN HERR.

The excitement of years of mystery, danger, furtive rendezvous, and secret codes...

During Florestan's aria, "Und spür ich nicht linde," leave the box and follow the hallway on the left until you reach backstage.
We'll be waiting...

ICH SEH' WIE EIN ENGEL IM ROSIGEN DUFT...

FOLLOW ME, THIS WAY.

WAIT HERE, PLEASE.

WIR HABEN NICHT VIEL ZEIT!

WHAT'D SHE SAY?

THAT WE DON'T HAVE MUCH TIME.

This time, due to the language barrier, G. couldn't do without my help.

DER BARON WAR KEIN SCHLECHTER MENSCH, EIN SCHMU... ...ABER...

THE BARON WASN'T A BAD MAN. YES, HE WAS A TRAFFICKER, ESPECIALLY WITH INFORMATION. BUT WE ALL NEEDED TO SURVIVE DURING THE WAR.

TIEF IM INNERN WAR ER SOGA... MENSCH... ANDEREN... ARISTOKRA... REICHISO...

DEEP DOWN, HE WAS EVEN A GOOD MAN, ALWAYS WILLING TO HELP OTHERS... AN ARISTOCRAT IN THE AUSTRO-HUNGARIAN TRADITION.

NOW THAT THEY'VE KILLED HIM, I DON'T KNOW WHAT WILL BECOME OF ME. I'M CZECH, YOU SEE. IF THE RUSSIANS GET ME, THEY'LL SEND ME BACK EAST.

JET... N... TSC... ...MEN, WERDEN SIE MICH IN DEN OSTEN ZURÜCKSCHICKEN.

ASK HER WHAT SHE WANTS.

DER BARON HAT MIR DIE DOKUMENTE, DIE SIE INTERESSIEREN, HINTERLASSEN, UND ICH BIN BEREIT, SIE IHNEN IM TAUSCH GEGEN EIN... ZU ÜBER...

SHE SAYS THAT THE BARON LEFT DOCUMENTS WITH HER THAT ARE OF INTEREST TO YOU AND THAT SHE'S READY TO GIVE THEM TO YOU IN EXCHANGE FOR A VISA FOR LONDON...

INGE, YOU NEED TO GO RIGHT NOW!

INGE! WAIT!

CHORUS ON STAGE!

WHEN CAN I SEE YOU AGAIN?

SPÄTER, LASS MICH IN RUHE!

GRAHAM!

LET HER GO. I'LL BE IN TOUCH.

MR. GREENE! I THOUGHT I MIGHT FIND YOU BACKSTAGE.

LEROY AND JONES, MY ASSISTANTS.

WELL, GOOD NIGHT THEN. I SUSPECT WE'LL BE SEEING EACH OTHER AGAIN VERY SOON.

WHENEVER YOU WANT, BILLY BUD.

ELIZABETH, I NEED THOSE DOCUMENTS!

WE SHOULD GO SEE BEAUCLERK FOR THE VISA.

LET'S LEAVE HIM OUT OF THIS. THERE MUST BE A FASTER WAY.

The next day, he asked me to drive him to Wien-Film, but insisted on seeing Hartl alone.

Confirmation that the "obliging Austrian" was indeed his contact with London.

WE'LL HAVE IT TOMORROW.

THE VISA? I'M IMPRESSED.

DON'T BE ANGRY WITH ME, ELIZABETH. YOU KNOW THE RULE: "YOU CAN'T REVEAL WHAT YOU DON'T KNOW."

I DON'T THINK I NEED A CERTIFICATE OF LOYALTY. I SACRIFICED A THEATRICAL CAREER TO SERVE MY COUNTRY IN THE SHADOWS.

ON PAPER, IT WAS THE SIMPLEST OF MISSIONS...

THIS MAN, HARPO, IS A HIGH-RANKING BUREAUCRAT.

THEY SUSPECT HE'S AN EASTERN SYMPATHIZER.

I WAS ASKED TO CHECK IT OUT. THAT'S IT.

That's it. "They give you matches without telling you that they're sending you to play on a powder keg?" I bit back my stinging reply...

We had visitors waiting in the Sacher lobby.

TAKE CARE OF THE GIRL. I NEED IDENTITY PHOTOS OF INGE...

MR. GREENE, SIR...

IT'S BEEN DAYS AND YOU HAVEN'T RESPONDED IN REGARDS TO THE MEETING WITH OUR BOOK CLUB...

VIENNA GOT TO ME, MR...

GRABBIT. I'M AFRAID OUR FRIEND HAS OTHER PRIORITIES THAN YOUR GATHERING. PLEASE EXCUSE US.

WE FISHED ONE OF YOUR ATTACKERS OUT OF THE DANUBE CANAL.

THE MAN WITH THE HORRIBLE HARELIP. EXECUTED WITH A .38 CALIBER BULLET IN THE CAR THAT HIT VON KURTZ.

DO YOU KNOW THAT MAN?

MR. BOOTS AND I GO WAY BACK.

I WAS INFORMED THAT THE POLICE WANTED TO BRING YOU IN TO IDENTIFY THE BODY. YOU WERE FRONT AND CENTER FOR VON KURTZ'S MURDER.

IN CASE YOU HAVEN'T TOLD ME EVERYTHING, NOW'S THE TIME.

IF MATTERS GET WORSE, MY DEPARTMENT CAN NO LONGER PROTECT YOU...

AT EASE, COLONEL. SOMETHING TELLS ME OUR FRIEND WON'T BE STAYING IN VIENNA FOR LONG.

AM I WRONG, MR. G.?

I THINK I HAVE ABOUT EVERYTHING I NEED FOR THE FILM.

EXCEPT FOR THE ENDING!

STORIES DON'T HAVE A BEGINNING OR AN END, BILLY BUD. WHERE THEY START AND FINISH IS ALWAYS AN ARBITRARY CHOICE BY THE AUTHOR.

And neither did I, especially since he had told me about the death of Rabe, the terrifying harelipped killer. I sensed the hand of my sweet Bud Boots behind that one.

COME IN.

The next day, our story swung into high gear. G. had no desire to find himself officially involved with von Kurtz's death.

At 08:00, a messenger from Wien-Film dropped off a package at the Sacher with a brand-new passport.

ILSE SMITH
BRITISH PASSPORT
E-PASS
I VLLC29

By 10:00, I had reached Inge's friend and had set up a rendezvous for later that morning, once again in the Russian zone.

INGE IS WAITING.

WHAT A FUN IDEA. IN WE GO, ELIZABETH!

HABEN SIE MEINEN PASS?

IF YOU HAVE MY DOCUMENTS...

DER BARON WOLLTE SIE IHNEN VERKAUFEN, ABER ICH BIN MIT DEM AUSWEIS ZUFRIEDEN.

SHE'S NOT ASKING YOU FOR MONEY. THE PASSPORT IS ENOUGH.

THAT'S VERY KIND OF HER. TELL HER THAT SHE IS NOW THE AUSTRIAN WIFE OF A CORPORAL SMITH AND SHE'S LEAVING TONIGHT TO JOIN HIM IN ENGLAND.

THANK YOU, SIR.

At noon, an unexpected and friendly visit.

YOU ENJOYED THE VIEW, I HOPE.

RUBBLE UNDER THE SUN... UNFORGETTABLE.

HOW ABOUT WE GO GRAB LUNCH?

ANOTHER TIME, BILLY BUD. I HAVE FAR TOO MUCH TO DO. I LEAVE VIENNA TOMORROW.

First piece of news.

DELIGHTED TO LEARN YOU'RE LEAVING. LONDON?

ROME. WITH A STOP IN PRAGUE.

PRAGUE?

A SIMPLE FORMALITY.

DO YOU KNOW WHAT'S IN THE BARON'S ENVELOPE?

MORE OR LESS.

VON KURTZ BELONGED TO AN EXFILTRATION RING FOR NAZI ELITES WITH TIES TO THE VATICAN.

THAT OLD REPROBATE? OF COURSE HE DID...

HE REDEEMED HIMSELF... WITH A GOOD DEED, IN FACT.

WHO'S THAT ENVELOPE GOING TO SAVE?

INGE SCHMIDT.

AND WHO'S IT GOING TO DOOM?

TOO EARLY TO SAY.

Afternoon: waiting again in front of Wien-Film.

"You know everything, but it's better if good old Hartl doesn't know that," chuckled G. before leaving me alone with my Player's and the leather smell of the Mercedes.

This time, he returned from Ali Baba's cave with a packed briefcase.

It was already dark when I dropped him at the Sacher.

He said he needed to finish some letters and pack his bags.

I still had work to do as well

Our goodbye dinner was cordial but brief. The plane to Prague was leaving early the next day.

Although I had hoped to hear more about his Czechoslovakian detour, I got little for my pains.

In return, I said nothing about my plans.

THANKS, ELIZABETH. I HOPE TO SEE YOU AGAIN IN LONDON.

BEAUCLERK?

AS EFFICIENT AS WIEN-FILM WHEN IT COMES TO VISAS, APPARENTLY.

MY PERSISTENT GUARDIAN ANGEL...

HEY, MR. G.! STILL ON THE FRONT LINE?

A COURTESY VISIT TO MY EDITOR IN PRAGUE.

SO NOTHING TO DO WITH THE FACT THAT CZECHOSLOVAKIA IS SLIPPING INTO THE HANDS OF THE REDS?

Ignoring Boots, G. settled into his seat and focused on his reading.

THE GOSPEL OF NICODEMUS?

NICODEMUS WAS THE THIRD MAN PRESENT WHEN CHRIST WAS PLACED IN HIS TOMB, ALONG WITH JOHN THE EVANGELIST AND JOSEPH OF ARIMATHEA.

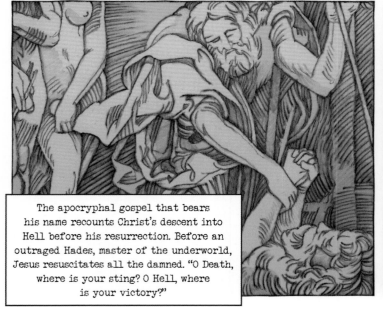

The apocryphal gospel that bears his name recounts Christ's descent into Hell before his resurrection. Before an outraged Hades, master of the underworld, Jesus resuscitates all the damned. "O Death, where is your sting? O Hell, where is your victory?"

THIS GOSPEL, WHICH DECLARED THE UNCONDITIONAL FORGIVENESS OF ALL SINS, DISPLEASED THE CHURCH FATHERS.

A FASCINATING THEOLOGICAL CONTRADICTION...

Prague — city of a hundred spires raised like broadswords toward a heavy sky...

...a city consumed by a leaden atmosphere...

...overtaken by a slow insurrection.

THE LAST BREACH IN MR. CHURCHILL'S DEAR "IRON CURTAIN" IS CLOSING BEFORE OUR EYES.

A HISTORICALLY DEMOCRATIC COUNTRY FALLS INTO MOSCOW'S CLAWS WITHOUT A SHOT BEING FIRED.

DID YOU RESERVE YOUR ROOMS?

I DIDN'T THINK IT WOULD BE NECESSARY AT THIS TIME OF YEAR.

HOTELS ARE ALWAYS FULL WHEN THERE'S A REVOLUTION.

Boots was right. However, G.'s notoriety got us two rooms in the attic.

The snowstorm and the silent crowds upon our arrival had made for an exhausting trip.

Once we were rested, it was too late to find a place to eat, either in the hotel or in Prague itself. But the one and only Boots had jumped into action.

BLACK MARKET!

MAKE DO WITH WHAT YOU HAVE.

HAVE YOU HEARD OF THE SALAMI TACTIC, MR. G.?

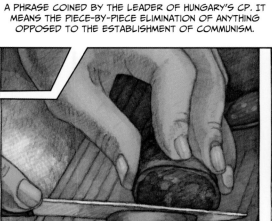

A PHRASE COINED BY THE LEADER OF HUNGARY'S CP. IT MEANS THE PIECE-BY-PIECE ELIMINATION OF ANYTHING OPPOSED TO THE ESTABLISHMENT OF COMMUNISM.

WHICH IS WHAT THE CZECH CP DID, BY LIQUIDATING THE DEMOCRATIC PARTY OF SLOVAKIA, AND THEN PROVOKING THE RESIGNATION OF LIBERAL MINISTERS.

THE HEROISM OF MEMBERS OF THE COMMUNIST RESISTANCE DURING LIBERATION EARNED THEM THE PEOPLE'S SYMPATHY, WHICH EXPLAINS THE CROWDS FLANKED BY PARTY MILITIAS.

WE'RE NOT IN VIENNA ANYMORE, MR. G. WHATEVER YOU'RE PLANNING ON DOING, I SUGGEST YOU EXERCISE THE UTMOST CAUTION.

I WON'T GET IN OVER MY HEAD.

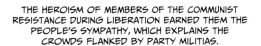

GOOD TO HEAR.

I WON'T HAVE TIME TO CHAPERONE YOU TOMORROW.

I'M INTERVIEWING THE SOVIET VICE MINISTER OF FOREIGN AFFAIRS AND STEINHARD, THE U.S. AMBASSADOR. IT APPEARS THAT THE WORLD HAS CHOSEN PRAGUE AS THE SITE FOR THE FINAL DUEL.

The next day, the crowds were still there.

JEDNOTOU PRACUJÍCÍCH K SOCIALISACI

"Rebels are growing on trees," said G. with a smile.

He was a charming character. They spoke in French, a language that was part of my repertoire.

YOU'VE ARRIVED IN DARK TIMES, MY FRIEND.

He had to meet with his editor (whom he specified was "Catholic") to talk business, which seemed a little incongruous in this climate of revolution.

The Catholic editor's office was near Parizska Street, where the old ghetto used to be.

THE SOVIET MACHINE IS GRINDING AWAY. OUR GREAT PRESIDENT BENEŠ WON'T LAST MUCH LONGER.

GOD ONLY KNOWS WHAT UNENDING WINTER MY POOR COUNTRY WILL SINK INTO THEN.

I was vaguely listening to them discussing the Czech edition of *The Power and the Glory* when a figure on the other side of the street startled me.

I held back my gasp. They had changed subjects.

ABOUT THAT PRIEST THAT YOU WANTED TO MEET...

FATHER JOZSEF.

And this one struck me as more edifying.

HE EXERCISES HIS MINISTRY IN ST. NICHOLAS PARISH. HE CAN SEE YOU AT YOUR CONVENIENCE.

THE EARLIER THE BETTER.

WHAT DID YOU SEE OUTSIDE, ELIZABETH?

I THOUGHT I GLIMPSED THE BESPECTACLED PHOTOGRAPHER FROM VIENNA.

WHAT DID OUR FRIEND BOOTS SAY? EVERYONE IS IN PRAGUE...

That was all we did that day. We returned to the Alcron Hotel as the faint rumble of revolution, interspersed with cries and shouts, swelled from the city.

The next day hit like a migraine. G. stayed locked up in his attic room working. He seemed to be waiting for something -- a sign or message.

I tried to go out, but after a few steps down streets overrun with hostile crowds, I turned around and went back to the hotel.

The ambience was different there. Press correspondents had swarmed the Alcron and the staff's revolutionary mood added to the joyful confusion that reigned between its walls.

Around 17:00, a clamor rose from Prague.

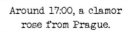

I found Boots in the lobby. He had just gotten back.

THE GOVERNMENT'S IN PRO-RUSSIAN HANDS. THEY'VE BEGUN TO ARREST THE OPPOSITION.

WHAT'S GOING TO HAPPEN?

IT'S HARD TO SAY. BUT THE COLD WAR IS TURNING TO ICE AND STALIN WILL BE SURE TO SEE IT THROUGH.

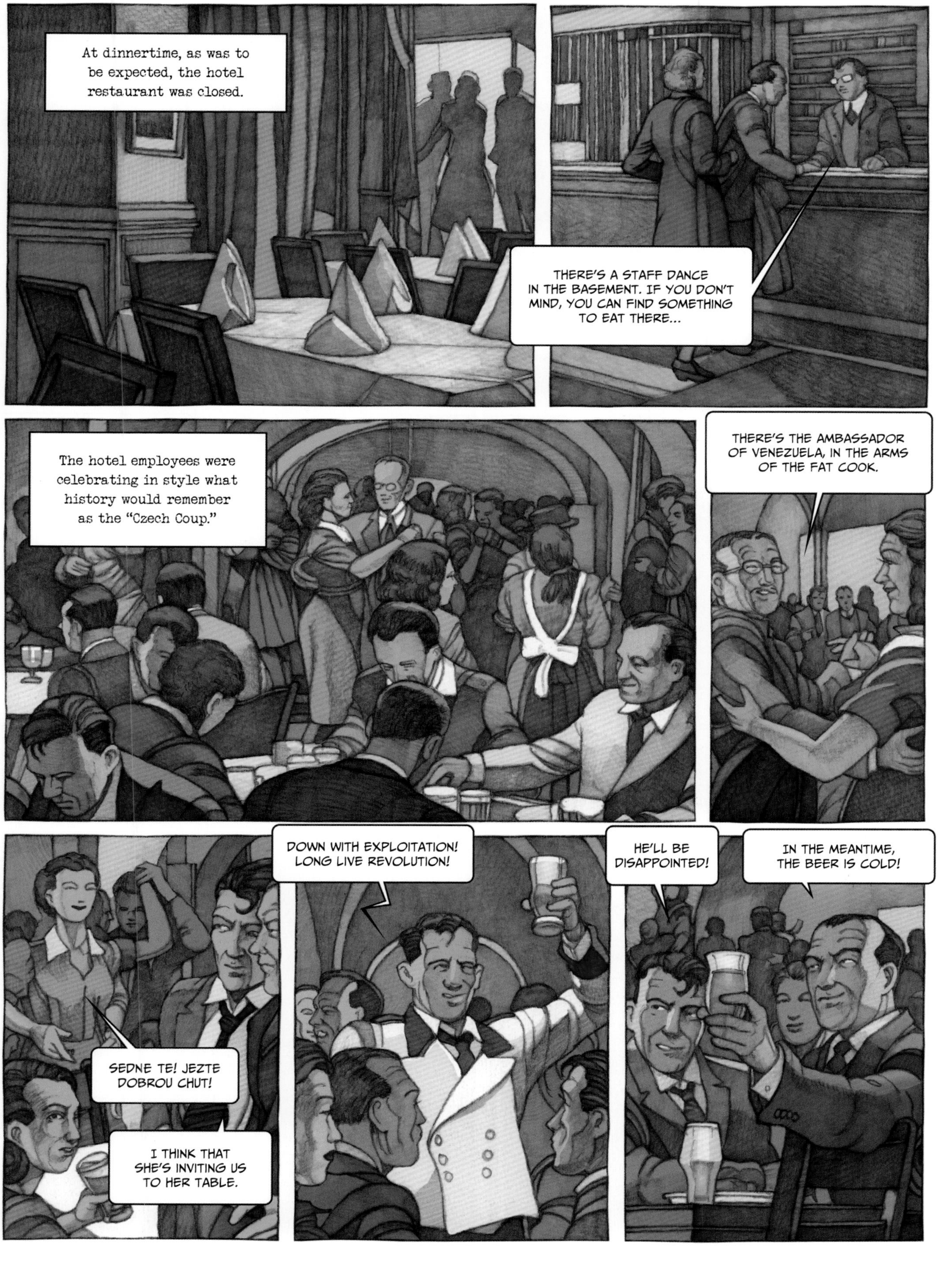
At dinnertime, as was to be expected, the hotel restaurant was closed.
THERE'S A STAFF DANCE IN THE BASEMENT. IF YOU DON'T MIND, YOU CAN FIND SOMETHING TO EAT THERE...
The hotel employees were celebrating in style what history would remember as the "Czech Coup."
THERE'S THE AMBASSADOR OF VENEZUELA, IN THE ARMS OF THE FAT COOK.
SEDNE TE! JEZTE DOBROU CHUT!
I THINK THAT SHE'S INVITING US TO HER TABLE.
DOWN WITH EXPLOITATION! LONG LIVE REVOLUTION!
HE'LL BE DISAPPOINTED!
IN THE MEANTIME, THE BEER IS COLD!

Beer obliging, the party was heating up. Before joining the farandole, I saw G. glance at his watch.

Two taxis were waiting along the deserted pavement. I saw G. leave in the first one.

I didn't think twice about the destination.

ST. NICHOLAS CHURCH... ERR... SANKTUS MIKULÁ...

CHRÁM SVATÉHO MIKULÁS E?

NOT WITHOUT ME, MISS LIZZY!

CHRÁM SVATÉHO MIKULÁS E!

CLOSED!

IF HE'S IN THERE, HE MAY HAVE GONE IN AROUND BACK.

WHATEVER YOU DO, DON'T MOVE. AND PUT THIS ON IF YOU DON'T WANT TO FREEZE TO DEATH.

BUT...

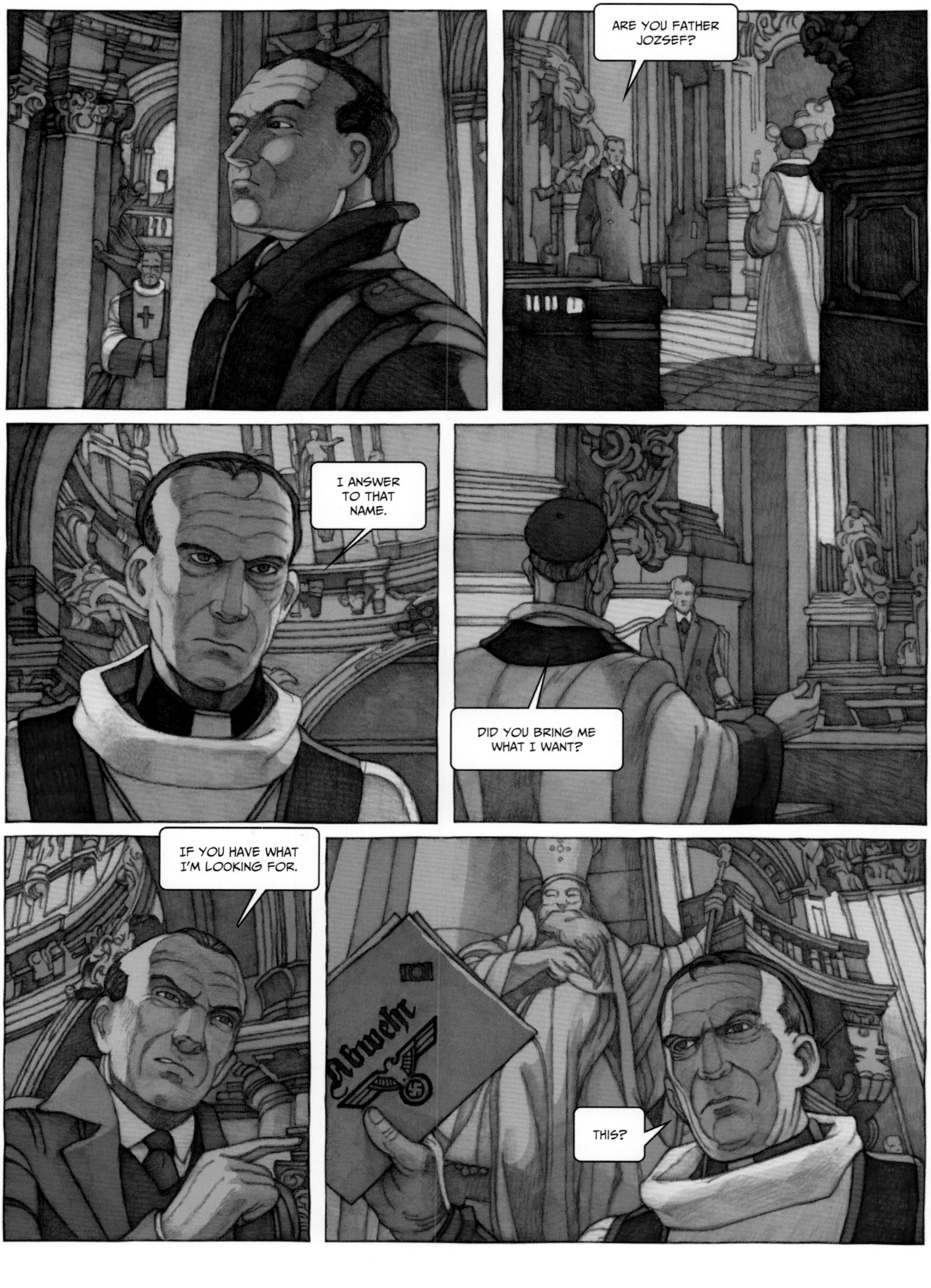
ARE YOU FATHER JOZSEF?
I ANSWER TO THAT NAME.
DID YOU BRING ME WHAT I WANT?
IF YOU HAVE WHAT I'M LOOKING FOR.
Abwehr
THIS?

IN THAT CASE, I HAVE YOUR SAFE-CONDUCT AND YOUR 30 PIECES OF SILVER.

I HAD NO CHOICE. IF I DID, BELIEVE ME THAT JUDAS'S ACT--

STOP JUSTIFYING YOURSELF, PADRE, AND BRING ME THAT FILE.

YOU AGAIN? YOU HAVEN'T LET ME OUT OF YOUR SIGHT SINCE THAT AMBUSH IN FRONT OF SMOLKA'S PLACE.

SMOLKA WAS A ROTTEN EGG. WE WERE AFRAID HE WOULD GIVE YOU WHAT THIS ONE WAS PLANNING TO SELL YOU.

BRING ME THE FILE, YOU NAZI!

NO!

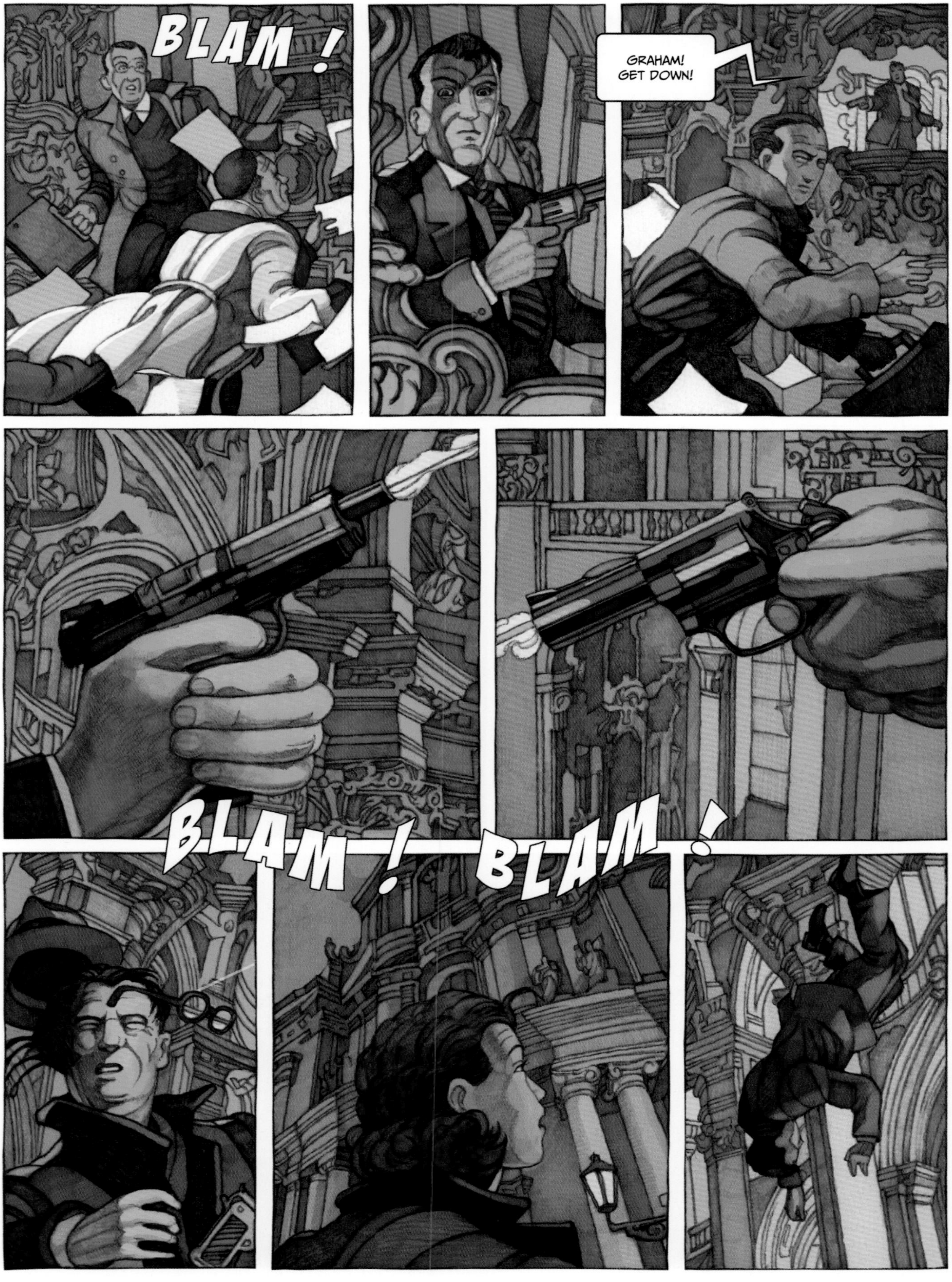
BLAM !
GRAHAM! GET DOWN!
BLAM ! BLAM !

Without thinking, I began running in the direction that Boots had taken.

It took me some time to find an entrance.

WHERE'S BOOTS?

DEAD. THEY KILLED EACH OTHER.

OH MY GOD! BUT WHY?

FOR THIS!

A FILE FROM THE NAZI SECRET SERVICE ABOUT HARPO'S SUPPOSED RECRUITMENT BY THE SOVIET NKVD IN VIENNA IN 1934.

THE PRIEST, EMBROILED WITH THE NAZIS, WAS USING IT TO BARTER FOR TRAVEL MONEY, IN DOLLARS, AND HIS EXFILTRATION THROUGH VATICAN CHANNELS.

A FOOL'S BARGAIN, IF YOU ASK ME.

JOZSEF WILL NEVER SEE ARGENTINA'S GENTLE SKIES AND THIS FILE IS A MESS OF LIES AND UNVERIFIABLE ALLEGATIONS.

I'M ENDING THE VICIOUS CIRCLE.

BY BETRAYING YOUR COUNTRY?

THREE MEN DIED TO GET AHOLD OF IT AND YOU'RE DESTROYING IT?

WHO AMONG US HAS NOT BETRAYED SOMEONE OR SOMETHING MORE IMPORTANT THAN A COUNTRY?

BETRAYAL, LOYALTY...

...WHAT MEANING DO THOSE WORDS HAVE IN A WORLD BUILT ON PILLAGING, MURDER, GENOCIDE, GAS CHAMBERS, THE NUCLEAR ERADICATION OF ENTIRE CITIES?

WHAT'S GOING TO HAPPEN NOW?

NOTHING.

NOW THAT PRAGUE'S THEIRS, THE RUSSIANS WILL START THE CLEAN-UP.

EXIT PHOTOGRAPHER.

BOOTS' DEATH WILL BE BLAMED ON THE REVOLUTION.

WHAT ABOUT THE NAZI PRIEST?

WHAT ABOUT ME? I COULD TALK...

I DON'T THINK YOU WILL. I'LL LEAVE YOU THIS AS A SOUVENIR...

...JOZSEF'S SAFE-CONDUCT. PROOF THAT THIS WASN'T A DREAM.

ISTITUTO TEUTON...

SANTA MARIA DELL...

TE ABSOLVO

WE WON'T SEE EACH OTHER AGAIN. I'M MEETING SOMEONE IN ROME TOMORROW.

THE LOVELY CAFRYN?

MY BETRAYAL. MY DEADLY SIN.

Over fifty years have gone by since that night in 1948 on that bridge of thirty statues straddling the Vltava.

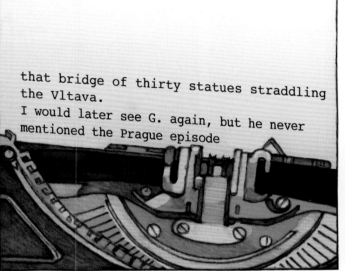

that bridge of thirty statues straddling the Vltava.
I would later see G. again, but he never mentioned the Prague episode

But it never left my mind. I kept my silence, as G. had predicted. And thus, I became an accomplice to his betrayal… if betrayal is the right word.

Because the truth that I uncovered as the years brought me the missing pieces, in the form of testimonials, letters, and biographies, was as subtle and complex as his dilemma.

WAYS OF ESCAPE · GREENE

THE HUMAN FACTOR GRAHAM GREENE

MY SILENT WAR KIM PHILBY

SOVIET INFLUENCE

Catherine W. or "Cafryn" was indeed waiting for him in Rome.

He dreamt of leaving his wife for her, but Catholics don't divorce.

He tackles that paradox in his novel *The Heart of the Matter*, published the year after his affair with Cafryn began.

And again three years later in *The End of the Affair*, which I think is one of his most beautiful books.

That's what writers do. They transform their transgressions, faults, and sorrows into art...

...and their art to stone.

That March in Anacapri, he bought a villa for next to nothing. Il Rosaio would serve as his refuge for the next forty years.

In September '49, our film received the Grand Prix at the 3rd Cannes Festival.

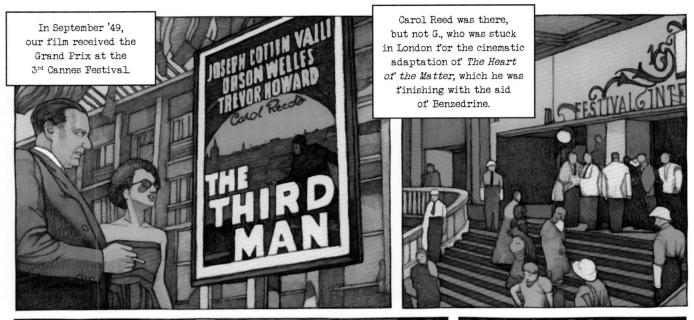

Carol Reed was there, but not G., who was stuck in London for the cinematic adaptation of *The Heart of the Matter*, which he was finishing with the aid of Benzedrine.

In the newly inaugurated Palais des Festivals, I discovered the end result of all our efforts and the inner workings of a writer's imagination.

I was struck by the fact that despite the extensive use of Smolka's articles on the sewers, and the penicillin black market, he wasn't even mentioned in the credits.

At the gala dinner at Eden Roc, Carol Reed told me that Smolka had been given 200 pounds sterling in exchange for his contributions and his silence.

But I would have to wait a few more years to discover the true secret of *The Third Man*.

In 1951, Burgess and Maclean, two diplomats with the Foreign Office, defected to the USSR. There were rumors of the existence of a "third man."

The American services suspected a high-ranking bureaucrat, delegated to Washington as a liaison agent between the CIA and FBI.

The expression obviously grabbed my attention.

But his name wasn't leaked to the press.

A "secret trial" was held in London. The "third man," suspected of being at the head of a network of Soviet moles, was interrogated by Helenus Milmo, a former prosecutor at the Nuremberg trials.

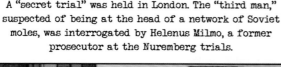

His findings, which were inconclusive, were buried.

In 1955, in response to a question about the "third man" in the House of Commons, Harold Macmillan affirmed that there was no reason to suspect Kim Philby of having betrayed his country's interests.

The name dropped.

It all clicked. Kim Philby. More precisely: Harold Adrian Russell Philby...

...H.A.R.P. Harpo!

Harpo. A cruel and poetic clown, whose madness and silence placed him out of reach of his human peers.

All of G.'s acerbic humor was in that code name...

In November 1955, Philby agreed to answer questions from the press.

CAN YOU TELL US WHEN YOU CUT OFF ALL RELATIONS WITH THE COMMUNIST PARTY?

THE LAST TIME I KNOWINGLY SPOKE TO A COMMUNIST WAS BACK IN 1934.

Were G. and I the only people in England who knew that this man was a shameless liar, that Philby was Harpo?

Everything fit. Philby had gone to Vienna in February '34 to cover the civil war pitting Socialists against Chancellor Dollfuss's "Austro-Fascists."

That was where the rebellious Cambridge student married Litzi Friedmann, the agent who had recruited him for the NKVD, in order to shield her from anti-Semitic militias.

A noble gesture that G. would have appreciated. The two men didn't meet until 1941, when G. joined MI6's section V, which was led by Philby.

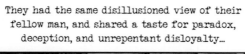
They had the same disillusioned view of their fellow man, and shared a taste for paradox, deception, and unrepentant disloyalty...

A GOOD OL' BOYS CLUB THAT REVOLVED AROUND DRINKING AND PLAYING AT WAR...

"Harpo" became a friend, a drinking buddy, the soul of the club that G. had told me about in Vienna...

Philby wasn't playing. As the head of British counter-intelligence, he was able to prevent the envoy sent by German generals plotting against Hitler -- Operation Valkyrie -- from contacting the Allies...

A way to delay the end of the War so that the Russians could reach Berlin first. The plot failed and the carnage lasted another year.

Did G. suspect his friend's role in that tragedy? He inexplicably resigned from MI6 a few days before the Normandy landings.

On January 23, 1963, Philby, who had become a reporter for *The Observer* in Beirut, disappeared. The USSR announced it had granted him political asylum in Moscow.

In his foreword to *My Silent War*, Philby's memoir published in 1968, G. reuses a phrase that I was the first to hear in that church in Prague.

My Silent War

"He betrayed his country." Yes, perhaps he did, but who among us has not committed treason against something or someone more important than a country?

The incredible truth struck me: the greatest post-war British film noir was a personal message to the traitor Philby…

In *The Third Man*, Holly Martins, a writer of Westerns, is reluctant to betray his friend Harry Lime, who he alone knows isn't dead.

He decides to do so only after seeing the horrific consequences of black market penicillin that forced Lime to disappear.

Harry is tracked through the sewers, surrounded, damned by the evil he sowed. Holly kills him, but out of compassion, to spare him the justice of men.

Unlike his American hero, G. didn't betray his friend Harpo. Undoubtedly, in his own strange way, he admired him too much for that.

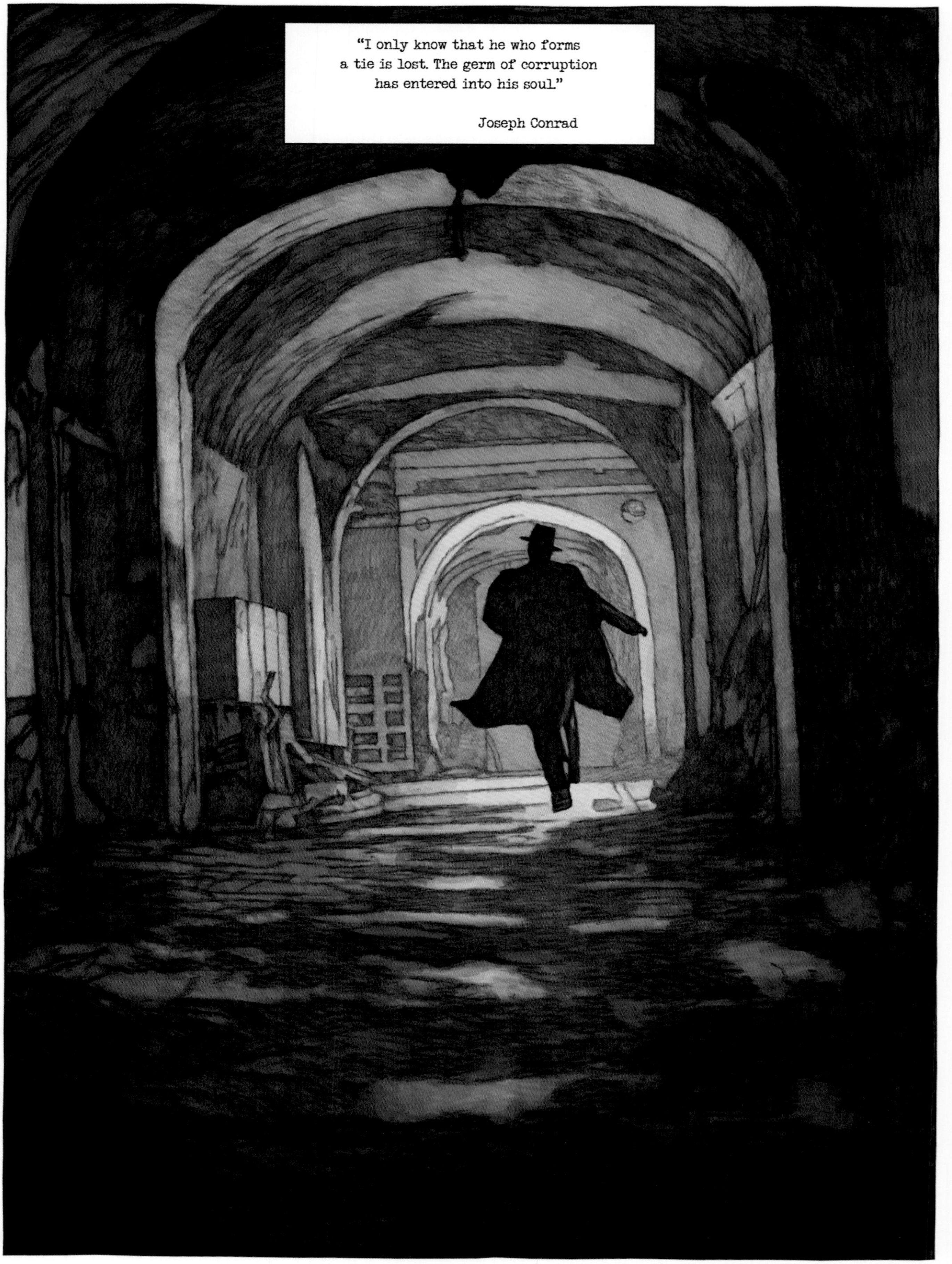
"I only know that he who forms a tie is lost. The germ of corruption has entered into his soul."
Joseph Conrad

GRAHAM GREENE THE ENEMY WITHIN

Novelist first and foremost, but also an essayist, journalist, editor, film critic, playwright, and scriptwriter; Graham Greene (1904-1991) left his mark on twentieth century literature. Twenty-six novels, four autobiographies, four travel journals, eight plays, ten film scripts, six news collections, fifteen collections of articles and essays, a fascinating biography of the 2nd Earl of Rochester – infamous debauchee of the Seventeenth century who, on the verge of death, converted to Catholicism – and even four books for children comprising a masterly body of work produced over sixty years of non-stop writing. Not to mention the flood of portraits, memoirs, essays, and correspondence that he inspired in his peers and contemporaries.

Contrary to those static writers who summon the world from their offices, Greene was an unrepentant globe-trotter. Liberia, Mexico, Sierra Leone, Malaysia, four trips to Uncle Ho's Indochina as special envoy – for the *Sunday Times*, for *Figaro*, and for *Paris Match* – Kenya during the Mau-Mau revolution, Castro's Cuba, a leper colony in the throes of death in Belgian Congo, Papa Doc's Haiti, Israel during the six day war, General Torrijo's Panama, Uruguay of the Tupamaros... All these hotspots and armed conflicts, rebellions, natural catastrophes shaking the world, attracted him like a magnet. Destinations picked to battle the boredom of the everyday by heading off in search of adventure, of inspiration and, being a manic depressive, of death. His whole life, this distant little nephew of Robert Louis Stevenson – author of *Treasure Island* and *Dr Jekyll and Mr Hyde* – sought pretexts to escape his insularity. In 1966, his exile became definitive. He settled in Antibes, which he only left twenty-five years later to end his days in Vevey, where Paul Morand, Charlie Chaplin, James Mason and many others all rest.

One could imagine that with all these travels – each one producing one or more books and myriad articles, so many encounters with remarkable (and famous) people, so many admirers, friends, rival writers – Greene's life would be as easy to follow as that of Tintin the reporter. Nothing of the sort. Like many creators before and after him, he went to pains to cover his tracks. Anything to shatter the image that the intelligentsia and public at large tried to confine him to ("Catholic writer" was the cliché he was most labeled with and to which he most strongly objected). This rage at never being when or where you were expected could invite comparison to a Picasso, or a Bob Dylan, even if unlike the latter, he would never receive the Nobel Prize for Literature*.

Preferring to manage himself the moving realities of his existence, he for a long time held biographers at a distance, discouraging any serious endeavor of the sort. In 1974, he nonetheless decided to appoint an academic, Norman Sherry – a little, nervous man, pernickety and impressionable, his very opposite, to whom he clearly announced: "I will live to see the first volume, but not the second, and you shall not follow the third." Everything Greene is in the cynicism of that prediction. All his acuity as well. To conjure the prediction into reality, Sherry would go as far as to leave the last phase of the last tome incomplete. He lived for twelve years after the publication in 2004. A miracle if one considers everything he'd endured – gangrene, tropical diabetes, temporary blindness – throughout the three decades necessary to successfully complete his biographical (and according to his detractors hagiographic) trilogy.

He religiously recreated every voyage of his model, to the point of almost never coming back from some of the rotten parts of the world to which his quest necessitated he travel. Swept along

*Greene missed out on the prize in 1980, two years after the release of his truly important novel, *The Human Factor*, to the benefit of the Polish poet Czeslaw Milosz. Explication by one of the jurors at the time: "Greene is too popular." Other days, other ways.

by his enthusiasm, he insisted heavily on Greene's chaotic sexual life, his dealings with alcohol and opium, his elastic relationship with lies and loyalty, attracting retribution from heirs, who accuse him of having betrayed the writer. Accusations most unjust. *The Life of Graham Greene* is a unique monument in the history of biography.

During that time, other less kind spirits took it upon themselves to untie the strings, the shadowy places, the false bottoms, and the acrobatics of this illusory life in order to uncover the prankster, the trickster, the professional fantasist behind the unruffled mask of this giant of British writing.

It's from reading one of these more probing works, *The Enemy Within*, by Michael Shelden, that the idea behind this very project was born. A book in which the unequivocal Greene I found was at once perfectly unpleasant and powerfully invigorating. A book which earned its author, also an academic, the title of 'literary terrorist' (especially from the loyal Sherry), he so viciously and ruthlessly attacks the image of Saint Greene. Many of the blows he delivers are low and more than questionable. Notably the accusations of antisemitism, targeting the 1930s stereotypes who populated Greene's first novels, of which he himself had the conscience to banish from his biography the most dubious in that respect, *The Name of Action*.

It's on the subject of the habits and the moral, religious, and political choices of his victim where Shelden is more convincing. He renders the portrait of a cheat that others disdain, pushed to surprising extravagances. Cruel jokes at the expense of friends, perverse and literary reprisals, such as when he charges, in *The Destructors*, a bunch of post-Blitz kids with demolishing the beautiful Georgian house of his wife Vivien, whom he was shamelessly cheating on with the illustrator of his children's books, Dorothy Craigie.

But the principal interest of this charged biography is the stark light it sheds on the most obscure traits of the novelist. His character of born-liar, for example, illustrated by the episode where the young man, son of Charles Henry Greene — highly puritanical governor of the boys' school in Berkhamsted where the adolescent drags his bipolar boredom around and cultivates his hatred for English public schools — comes up with morbid games of Russian Roulette for himself. This confidence served to feed his first public image, that of a young tragic-romantic Werther. And little does it matter when we learn much later that there weren't any bullets in the cylinder.

And so his complicated relationship with sex and religion (superbly exposed in his novel *The End of the Affair*). At twenty-six, Greene decided to turn his back on Anglican confession, too tepid for his taste, to embrace the more complex and tumultuous Catholic faith. Father Trollope baptized him in 1926. "I had to find a religion to measure my evil against," he would declare twenty-five years later. In 1940 he attracted more than just a frown from the Vatican with his novel *The Power and the Glory*, portrait of a craven priest, weak, self-destructive, illegitimate father, in search of redemption in a Mexico given over to a bloody anti-clerical wave. And in 1946, when Catherine Walston, a rich and beautiful American, asked Greene to become the godfather to her own conversion to Catholicism, he accepted, sent his wife in his stead to the baptism, and hastened to make a mistress out of his new goddaughter.

Shelden relates in detail the couple's walks in the Italian countryside and how their visits to churches would culminate in sexual ecstasy behind altars. In truth, Greene's faith is first and foremost a fantastic store of images, of parables and paradoxes which serve to sharpen his metaphors of the human tragedies which were his novels.

And so with spying. 'The novelist is a spy,' Greene would often repeat through his work. Lover of secrets, an obsessive curiosity for the lives of others, a fascination for shifting loyalties, all in the name of better learning the seduction. The profession was already well represented in the family, starting with his uncle, Sir William Graham Greene, who contributed at the end of the nineteenth century to the creation of the Naval Intelligence Department, the intelligence service of the Royal Navy. Or his older brother Herbert, spy in the service of the Imperial Japanese Navy in the 1930s and double agent for the British and Americans. Or Hugh, his cadet, whose role as correspondent for the *Daily Telegraph* in the Reich's Berlin concealed other less legitimate activities. Or Benjamin Greene, one of his cousins, suspected – and officially accused – to have been an agent and political agitator in the pay of the Nazis. To paraphrase Oscar Wilde, 'To have a spy in the family can be regarded as bad luck, to have several looks more like vice.' On the eve of the Second World War, Elizabeth, the author's younger sister, joined MI6. In 1941, she recruited her brother who received the designation 59200. He first exercised his talents in West Africa, in the quagmire of Freetown, where he experimented with the joys of confabulation – which were at the heart of the profession which would later serve him in creating the magnificent portrait of the pathological liar spy in *Our Man in Havana* – and then Section V in London, charged with the Lusitanian regions, under the orders of a certain Kim Philby.

Countless pieces on this complex man, who wrote *The Man Within,* reveal a powerful romantic figure, a life spotted with gray areas, caltrops, fake tracks, which make an irresistible invitation for the imagination to run away with.

In the end, one question remains: Who (or what) was Graham Greene? Saint or demon? One can say that all the good in the man resides in his work; in the incredible empathy of the author for his most tortured characters. In equity, honesty, the accuracy of touch he brings to the most lurid of situations. In his tenderness for the weak, the oppressed, the lost, the wild and naked caught up in forces whose monstrous indifference grinds them down. In his pity for poor sinners, a pity always threatened, but forever rekindled. Finally in his humor; the only British trait present in his nature that he would never renounce. A genius, without fail. Like other great writers, like Simenon, an examiner of the soul so concerned with examining, re-examining, dissecting and autopsying every facet of the human creature that *The Man Within* ended up containing everything defining the human: puritanical, depraved, lucid, gullible, terrorized, heroic, romantic, pragmatic, sadistic, masochistic, mystical, materialist, greedy, self-sacrificing, fraternal and compassionate, cruel and misanthropic, tormented by loyalty and apostle to betrayal...
    The complex man.
    The complete man.

ELIZABETH MONTAGU THE HONORABLE REBEL

The real Elizabeth Montagu – daughter of Douglas-Scott Montagu, second Baron Montagu of Beaulieu – was thirty-eight when she welcomed Graham Greene to Vienna in early February 1948 for the initial research for the film *The Third Man*. She was no longer, as she says, "a girl." But there dwells in her an innocence, a petulance, a dignified callback to a Hitchcockian, English period heroine, a mischief and anti-conformism perceptible even in her memoirs, *The Honorable Rebel*, written in her last days.

At her birth, on September 26th, 1909, nothing could predict the adventurous life that awaited Elizabeth. Heir in waiting to the title and lands of her family, she was prepared for the life of an aristocrat, future mistress of Beaulieu Abbey, Hampshire. At nine years old, she lost her mother, struck down by the Spanish Flu pandemic which ravaged the world post war. The arrival of a half-brother, Edward, ripped away the destiny written for her. In virtue of the conventions which governed the transfer of noble titles, the first son of John Montagu became the legitimate successor. He would remain Baron of Beaulieu until his death in 2015.

Freed of her obligations, the young girl cast off her shackles and threw herself headlong into a theatrical career. She ended up in London, on the stages of the West End. She could also be heard in BBC dramas. Shoed with the same soles of wind as Greene, she would spend the majority of the 1930s wandering across Europe, studying music in Switzerland, witnessing the rise of Nazism in Germany, meeting along the course of her peregrinations many important European writers. She found the time, between two escapades, to become the personal assistant to the conductor Arturo Toscanini, and help the producer of classical English music Walter Legge found the Philharmonic Orchestra. When war broke out, she refused a job offer with London's *Times* to instead drive an ambulance on the French front. She surprised her family by staying on the continent when the British evacuated their troops in 1940. After a clandestine period, during which she caught serious pneumonia in Angoulême, she managed to flee to Switzerland, just barely escaping the claws of the Gestapo.

A refugee in Zürich, Elizabeth reconnected with the theatre. While she endeavored to assemble a group of English speakers for a comedy by Somerset Maugham, she met an American comedienne expatriated to Switzerland who recruited her for the spy network which Allen Dulles, the head of the American Office of Strategic Services (OSS), established in Bern, close to enemy lines. She signed without hesitation. Her first mission was to interrogate the vice-consul of the German legation in Zürich, the doctor Hans Bernd Gisevius, opposed to Hitler's politics, and translate the imposing manuscript which he'd snuck out of Germany, unveiling the sinister aims of the Third Reich.

These months of interviews shed light on the best-kept secrets of the Nazis, including the development of the V2 destined to destroy London, leading to the allied bombing of the factory in Peenemünde where they were being made. They also revealed the existence of the June 20th, 1944 plot by generals against Hitler, which would go down in history as Operation Valkyrie. Elizabeth also had a hand in the first report out of Treblinka, detailing the horrors of the extermination camp in Poland.

After the war, transformed by her experiences, having become a progressive and internationalist, the young aristocrat began a career in cinema, as script writer and lead dialogue writer. In 1948, she found herself in Austria on behalf of Sir Alexander Korda's London Films. It's he who tasked her with receiving and acting as guide to Graham Greene, when the author came to Vienna to document the film they were preparing together.

Strangely, Greene doesn't even mention her name in the laconic telling of this time, which takes up five pages in his autobiographical *Ways of Escape*, released in England in 1980. He complains of "long solitary nights in the bars and night clubs" of the occupied city. Conversely, she affirms in her own memoirs being dragged around "the most sordid and lugubrious places in Vienna," Greene taking a cheeky pleasure in trying to shock her. Thus she discovered that the Oriental Club was in fact a brothel concealed beneath the benign appearance of a cabaret (she was also behind the famous visit to the sewers which would furnish the cornerstone of the film – the rat anecdote is straight from her book). Reminiscing on this episode in the fading light of her life, she didn't seem to hold Greene's behavior against him. She did however express some surprise that such a fervent Catholic could lower himself to such practices.

Surrounded by suitors and in spite of many liaisons, Elizabeth remained celibate up until 1962, the year that, at 52, she married Colonel Arthur Varley, dominating figure in the world of advertising, son of a poor pastor, hoisted to the summit by sheer strength. The couple settled in Hewton, the Victorian home of the Varleys in Devon, which overlooks the river Tamar and offers a spectacular view of nearby Cornwall. Of these cloudless days of happiness, Elizabeth stated that they were the perfect culmination to a vagabond life. She would end her days in Beaulieu Abbey, where she passed on May 6th, 2002.

The Honorable Rebel appeared a year later and, in 2015, became a British film production halfway between biopic and adventure movie. It's Diana Rigg, the immortal Emma Peel from the series *The Avengers*, who lends her voice to the narration. Confirmation that the honorable Elizabeth Montagu of Beaulieu, aristocrat, actress, adventurer, spy, free woman, was destined since the beginning to become a heroine of fiction.

THE THIRD MAN

"The writer is at heart a sort of criminal deprived of conscience. How many must die at his hand without the assassin remembering?" – GRAHAM GREENE

Graham Greene's relationship with cinema started early. In 1931, the 27-year-old writer was in trouble with Heinemann, his editor. The successive failures of *The Name of Action* and *Rumor at Nightfall*, his second and third novels, after the esteemed success of the first one, *The Man Within*, cast doubt on his continued career. The publishing house had invested a lot in him and expected substantial returns. Three years before Agatha Christie, he seized on the most mythical train in Europe, the Orient Express, to set a thrilling intrigue. With forty thousand copies sold in the first year, the book delivered him a future. What's more, Hollywood got involved. 20th Century Fox gave him £1,500 (a considerable sum for the period) for the rights to adapt it to screen. His was greatly disappointed to discover, several years later in a cinema in Tenerife, the level to which the studio had sugar-coated his story to make a trifle on rails. Never mind. He had measured the economical potential of the Seventh Art art and his interest prevailed. Between 1934 and 2010, 33 movies would be adapted (by him and others) from his novels and news pieces, to which one must add pretty much the same number of television adaptations.

His relationships with film studios, however lucrative, were not always excellent. A film lover since his studies at Oxford – where he gave his first critique for the *Oxford Outlook*, the literary review for the college – Greene suggested to the *Spectator*, a large conservative weekly paper for London, he take charge of the cinematographic rubric. His first article appeared on July 5th, 1935, dedicated to *The Bride of Frankenstein*, the masterpiece by James Whale, starring Boris Karloff. The collaboration would last for four and a half years, during which he saw 424 films and gave his verdict on every one. He preferred Laurel and Hardy to Chaplin, gushed over the mysteries of Greta Garbo and the understated style of Gary Cooper. He also regularly lashed out at the works of Alexander Korda, affirming his contempt of flashy tastes.

In 1937, Greene had a hand in the creation of *Night and Day*, London's answer to the *New Yorker*. Its mocking spirit and tendency toward provocation hastened its premature end. In the October 28th issue his critique of *Wee Willie Winkie** – Twentieth Century Fox's latest movie featuring Shirley Temple, the nine year old megastar – appeared. He wrote: "The owners of a child star are like leaseholders — their property diminishes in value every year (...) Miss Shirley Temple's case, though, has peculiar interest: infancy with her is a disguise, her appeal is more secret and more adult (...) Her admirers — middle aged men and clergymen — respond to her dubious coquetry, to the sight of her well-shaped and desirable little body, packed with enormous vitality, only because the safety curtain of story and dialogue drops between their intelligence and their desire."

The scandal might have been contained if the redaction hadn't thought it a good idea to flood London in red leaflets announcing "Sex and Shirley Temple." The slander trial and condemnation which followed cost the author £500 and the magazine £3000. In December *Night and Day*, already financially fragile, sunk with all hands. Greene was advised to try and be forgotten. He left for Mexico and began the research which would lead to *The Power and The Glory*, his first literary triumph. Nothing was lost.
Meanwhile, the skillful Korda, who recognized talent and knew how to rally such an enemy to

*Directed by John Ford, whom Greene accused in the article of being 'horrifyingly competent.'

his cause, got in touch and invited Greene to work for him. Alexander Korda, born Sandor Laszlo Kellner in Hungary at the end of the nineteenth century, had already made 25 films in his country before he emigrated to Vienna, Berlin, Paris, and then Hollywood. He spoke Yiddish, German, French, and English. Ten years later, he became the first filmmaker to be knighted by the Queen, an accomplishment in a time when foreigners (Jews particularly) were subject to every prejudice. His biggest successes as a producer were *The Four Feathers* (1939), *The Thief of Baghdad* (with Conrad Veidt and Sabu, 1940) and...*The Third Man*.

In 1936, Korda offered Greene £1000 for a script called *The Green Cockatoo*. This sentimental thriller was a failure, but the producer, far from discouraged, plowed more money the next year into an adaptation of John Galsworthy, author of *The Forsythe Saga*. It didn't find its audience either, despite the on-screen presence of the golden couple Laurence Olivier and Vivien Leigh. In 1940, he paid out £2000 for the rights to *The Power and The Glory*, which he would later hand over to John Ford. The professional relationship between Korda and Greene didn't prove fruitful until after the war, with the addition of a new player, the producer Carol Reed. The latter had 20 movies under his belt by the time he joined Greene on *The Fallen Idol*. The result was well received by both critics and public alike. Enough for Korda to finance a new project. This time, he stretched to £9000 for an original script which Reed would direct.

A few conditions were attached to the fantastic contract. The film had to be a thriller and take place in Vienna, the martyred occupied city in which the producer could see considerable dramatic potential and, crucially, where he held blocked funds in an Austrian subsidiary, Wien-Film.

That's why, on a freezing day in February 1948, Greene set off for Wien-Schwechat, the Viennese airport, where the petulant Miss Montagu was waiting. He had only a very vague idea for his story – a single sentence describing the meeting in a London avenue between a man and the friend he buried several days ago – and was relying on his time in Vienna to furnish him with the struts and material. If official literature documents in detail the success of this trip, we find plenty more interpretations in the unauthorized biographies. A series of proven facts tends to suggest a secret mission hidden behind this research trip.

Firstly there's the confirmed involvement of Sir Alexander Korda with the world of espionage. This colorful person (who Greene would caricature, not without affection, in the comic novel *Loser Takes All*, with the excellent strokes of a tycoon nicknamed GOM, "The Grand Old Man") who had, since the 1930s, lent his formidable network of influence and his talent for organization to the service of His Majesty. If his patriotism was above suspicion, his sense of business didn't suffer. Many political personalities (including Winston Churchill, credited with an untraceable role) appeared on the payrolls of London Films. The return in investment allowed him to produce some of the most beloved films of English cinema of the time. Orson Welles would say of him, "He really wanted to be the prince Metternich*, and he stuck to the role better than Prince Metternich himself."

There's also Colonel John Codrington, former agent of Claude Dansey, the vice-director of the British secret service during the war. His role at the heart of Korda's organization was to facilitate the movement of London Films personnel abroad, during an era in which the British government enforced heavy restrictions in that respect. It's he who orchestrated Greene's stay in Vienna and

*Prince Klemens Wenzel von Metternich (1773-1859), diplomat and statesman of the Austro-Hungarian Empire, arranged with France, in order for peace, the marriage between Napoleon and the young arch-duchess Marie Louise.

allowed him to reach, without hindrance, a Prague stuck behind the Iron Curtain, an unforeseen (and to this day unexplained) extension to his journey.

There's also Peter Smolka. Born in Vienna, the man had a pretty foggy London past (reporter for the *Daily Express*, special envoy for *The Times* in Central Europe, chief of the Russian section for the British Ministry of Information, tasked with pro-Soviet propaganda) when Greene paid him a visit at Elizabeth Montagu's instigation. Whilst permanent correspondent for *The Times* in the capital of the Habsburgs, he is, they say, the one who was most familiar with the underbelly of Vienna. A windfall for an author in search of sensational anecdotes with which to feed his script. At the time of their meeting, Smolka handed him a manuscript containing documents on the trafficking of penicillin, which would become Harry Lime's trademark, and on the sewer network used by the underworld during occupation by the Allied Powers, where *The Third Man* would resolve itself. Unsurprisingly, Greene didn't mention his name or that of Elizabeth, in the five famous pages which he dedicated to the genesis of the film. He affirmed that it was Colonel Beauclerk, chief of the information services of the Allied Commission, who he owed for the information on the penicillin and sewers. We would discover later that Smolka (aka Peter Smollett) had, since 1933, been an agent of the Russian NKVD, codenamed "ABO."

It's Smolka, in fact, who made the link with the last ace in this hand of spies, Kim Philby. The two men met in London in 1933 and returned to Vienna a year later. It's hard to say who recruited whom for the Russians, sources disagree on the subject. What is certain is that Smolka presented Litzi Friedmann to Philby. The young woman already worked for Russian intelligence. The Englishman – in Vienna as a journalist to cover, and at the same time support, the workers' insurrection of February 1934 against the Austrofascist government of Chancellor Dollfuss – married Litzi, enabling her to escape the henchmen who were tracking her. She was Jewish and the Austrian authorities shared Hitler's views on the subject.

Harold Adrian Russell Philby was a pure product of the Group from Cambridge, formed by students of wealthy families converted very early to Marxism. He joined MI6 in June 1940, the ideal position to secretly serve his masters in the Kremlin. In 1942, Greene was attached to Section V, of which Philby was head. A mutual admiration blossomed between the two. Yet, in June 1944, the novelist suddenly resigned from the Service, several days before D-Day. To go from there to say that he suspected the activities of his direct supervisor, is not a huge leap of faith. Though even the faithful Norman Sherry has questions on the subject. In Volume 2 of his biography, he writes: "Greene once told me that if he had known that Philby was a Soviet counterspy, he "might have allowed him 24 hours to flee as a friend, then reported him." Would he really have done so, this admirer of betrayal?

The premise for this very work is founded on that uncertainty. The idea is that the visit to Vienna, for the film *The Third Man,* ostensibly serves as a cover to uncover Philby's tracks. That, by a bewildering twisting of fact and fiction, Philby would inherit in 1962, the year of his defection to the USSR, that same title of "Third Man." He was in effect the third mole to be unmasked in the network planted deep in the heart of British intelligence, after Burgess and Maclean whom he helped to escape before becoming himself the most famous defector in the Cold War. Six years later, he published (from Moscow, where he lived thereafter) his memoirs as a spy, *My Silent War*. The introduction, provided by his friend Graham Greene, makes a lot of noise. "An honest book, well written, sometimes funny. He betrayed his country, yes, possibly that is the case, but who amongst you hasn't committed treason on encountering something or someone more important than a country?" A comment which didn't go down very well amongst the circles of authority, regarding a man whose clandestine dealings led to the loss of freedom, or deaths, of several hundred agents and delayed the end of the war by several months.

By putting these facts together, it becomes tempting to see *The Third Man* as a personal message addressed to Philby: "I saw you, I won't inform on you, but now you know that I know." After all, friendship, treason, pardon, and redemption are all themes around which the film revolves.

One last, more subjective, element supports this literary license. With every viewing of this masterpiece by Greene and Carol Reed, I am struck by the gesture of Harry Lime's porter, announcing the death of the tenant to his friend, Holly Martins, only just arrived in Vienna. Speaking of Hell and Heaven, the man successively points with his finger to the ceiling and then the floor. Such an inversion could not be a mistake in filming. If you interpret it as one of the keys the author loved to litter his works with, everything becomes coherent. The war has reversed everything. Harry Lime appears like the figure of a fallen god, purveyor of tampered medicine (cut penicillin), hiding in the sewers to escape from his creature's wrath. A theological provocation very in keeping with Greene, emphasized even by the title itself. The third man could, in effect, be Nicodemus who, in the gospel which bears his name, was present at the entombment of Jesus Christ alongside John the Baptist and Joseph of Arimathea. To know that this gospel was omitted from the New Testament by the heads of the Church because it covers Our Saviour's descent into hell, offers salvation to the righteous who had died since the beginning of time, contradicts the founding tenets of Christianity. We at the very least have the gesture of the hardworking writer, Holly Martins, friend and humble disciple of Lime, who ends up dispatching his master, half in disgust at the horrors the other has perpetuated, half to save him from the damnation which awaits him. Greene's gesture, more prosaic, was to write what would remain the greatest European noir movie post World War II.

– Jean-Luc Fromental
Paris, January 2017

AFTERWORD

Graham Greene, whose shade Jean-Luc Fromental has ingeniously conjured in this tale, was a surprisingly complex, subtle, and large enough character to allow innumerable interpretations of him. My sense is that of almost anything one says about him, the opposite is also true. He was rightly said to be very private and would give no interviews, yet he allowed a great many to genuinely interested journalists. The reason everyone knew so much about his often misinterpreted infidelities or sexual life during his life, is because he was open to those concerned privately, and in general terms publicly. A blackmailer would have been way too late to threaten him. He was certainly the most widely generous person I knew of in my life but also, occasionally, aggressively denying. He could be intuitively empathetic in a way that captured women and men for life, and underlies the appeal, to many, of his books. Yet he did appear wounding and seemingly heartless to some of the women he loved; it was one of the few things about which he felt guilt. Even so, nearly all remembered him not as a predator, but as a warm friend to whom they remained loyal for life – as in a converse way did his wife, Vivien, who felt permanently wounded by his loss.

An instance of this complexity is his close friendship with Kim Philby, with whom Graham worked in SIS during the war, who appears in this story of the Prague Coup. Philby was deeply damaging to British interests. My father, married to Graham's youngest sister, Elisabeth, both also in SIS, was involved in the operation Jean-Luc describes, when discussing Graham's resignation from Section V of SIS. Many agents died – betrayed by Philby. My father was furious at Graham's intro to Philby's memoirs. Graham would not have known of the betrayal involved in the operation when he wrote it, but he would have known that such things could be the consequence of betrayal. He never praised the betrayal. How are these things to be put together?

Graham's defense of Philby's integrity and their friendship is seen by many as a foolish blip. Another great friend, Nicholas Elliott, my godfather, who actually did give Philby 24 hours to get away (to avoid embarrassment to MI6), confronted him. But it was not a blip. A few months later Graham was awarded the Shakespeare Prize and gave a lecture, published as *The Virtue of Disloyalty*, criticizing Shakespeare for failing to defend a fellow poet, Southwell, tortured and killed by Queen Elizabeth, but instead eulogizing the establishment. "It has always been in the interests of the State to poison the psychological wells…to restrict human sympathy," as he said. Years later Graham and Philby corresponded and met in Russia. Graham passed to my father every letter he sent to or received from Philby – as Philby did to the KGB. Were they being triple agents or just cleverly clearing a space for friendship by reassuring the gatekeepers? There seems to have been nothing significant in the letters.

Disloyalty to country, church, or government in favor of a higher loyalty to a human loving response (sometimes expressing the love of God), recognizing our often appalling extremity – which many preferred not to see and called Greeneland – is a thread through many of his books, as in *The Quiet American*. He would betray anything lesser for that. For him it would seem, as it did for many at that earlier time when the Soviet Union was an ally, that Philby's loyalty to a society that sought to end class and the abuse of power had integrity, and he took no money for his betrayals. Graham saw no reason to betray friendship to be loyal to the Soviet Union, Western governments, or the Church, who all betrayed their own ideals and abused their various human flocks.

Jean-Luc may have a quote that will prove me wrong but, even so, I don't think he preferred Karl to Harpo. To my mind humor, as Jean-Luc displays in this speculative thriller (which may well have amused Graham), ran like distant laughter through much of his serious writing, like the sound of vitality as in *Travels With My Aunt,* or like the gurgle of a sewer as in *The Third Man.* Perhaps a practical joke is not so far off from a good plot. Even his tale of the cowardly, drunken priest, with illegitimate child, in *The Power and the Glory*, who yet epitomizes God's mission of love to souls in extremity better than the edifices and officers of formal religion, punctures the pretensions of power. No wonder it was banned by the Vatican for a time. This appears again, decades later, in the holy 'fool' Quixote. Laughter has the sharpest point. When I was young I found this theme of God's love difficult. Though I am still an atheist, I am aware enough now to find it one of Graham's crucial dissidences.

Perhaps the facts we choose to recognize about a life or a time are bricks in a working model of reality we each construct. Even when sound, they can make an ill-built dwelling. The biography of Graham by poor Michael Shelden, perhaps frustrated at being denied access to source material by family and friends (merely attempting to honor Graham's promise of exclusivity to Norman Sherry), venomously distorted facts, not always sound, into fantastical shapes, "…to substantiate your stream of scurrilous allegations, including murder," as President Jimmy Carter put it to Shelden in disappointment. To make a good story or biography on a real figure we have to let them evidence their own life unselfishly. Unlike Shelden's humorless book, and perhaps with something of the delightful comedy of Tom Stoppard in *Rosencrantz and Guildenstern are Dead*, Jean-Luc Fromental, without denying himself speculation, does so. He inserts with great dexterity into a possible chapter of Graham's still half-written biography, a possible story, and many possible moments that might have been sources for Graham's book and film, *The Third Man.* It is witty and thrilling and potentially revealing. It could count as one of Graham's "entertainments." Bringing the remarkable Elizabeth Montagu, about whom I knew little, into the story is especially intriguing. In it they seem to be a different generation, but were in fact only five years apart. I wished they had fallen in love. But Graham remains loyal to someone, I can't remember whom at this point! And Jean-Luc has her find someone else.

As a family member I have no superior knowledge of Graham, though perhaps a particular sort of knowledge. Some have investigated, like assiduous sleuths, the details and meanings of his life, hunting their quarry to death. Jean-Luc is clearly deeply versed in all things Graham but, happily, many other things too. He lets his subject live. I do not recognize everything in his story or in his background material. But he has immersed himself in it with the integrity of one who wishes to let a life reveal itself. And the whole creates an echo of laughter that Graham might have enjoyed. Though with Graham one could never be sure.

– Nicholas Dennys

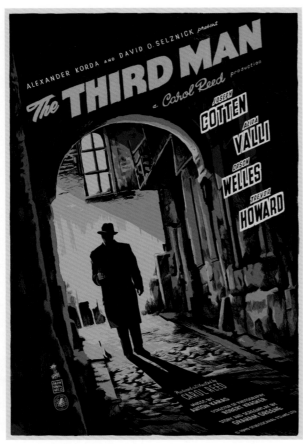

Art by Francesco Francavilla

WORLD PREMIERE, SEPTEMBER 1949
DIRECTED BY **CAROL REED** SCREENPLAY
BY **GRAHAM GREENE** • **ALEXANDER KORDA** •
CAROL REED
PRODUCED BY **CAROL REED** • **ALEXANDER
KORDA** • **DAVID O. SELZNICK** • **HUGH PERCEVAL**
FOR LONDON FILM PRODUCTIONS AND BRITISH
LION FILM CORPORATION
MUSIC BY **ANTON KARAS** WITH THE AUSTRIAN
ZITHER • PHOTOGRAPHY **ROBERT KRASKER**

JOSEPH COTTEN HOLLY MARTINS • **ORSON
WELLES** HARRY LIME • **ALIDA VALLI** ANNA
SCHMIDT • **TREVOR HOWARD** MAJOR CALLOWAY
• **BERNARD LEE** SERGEANT PAINE • **WILFRID
HYDE-WHITE** CRABBIN • **PAUL HÖRBIGER**
KARL, HARRY'S PORTER • **ERNST DEUTSCH**
THE 'BARON' KURTZ

GRAND PRIX WINNER CANNES FESTIVAL 1949 • BAFTA
FOR BEST BRITISH FILM 1949 • OSCAR FOR BEST
PHOTOGRAPHY 1951 • THIS FILM HAS BEEN VOTED
FIRST PLACE IN A LIST OF THE ONE HUNDRED BEST
BRITISH FILMS BY THE BRITISH FILM INSTITUTE

THE THIRD MAN MOVIE

The American Holly Martins, obscure pulp writer, arrives in Vienna at the instigation of his friend Harry Lime, who has promised lucrative affairs. On his arrival, Lime is dead, run over by a car. Martins decides to investigate and unmask the killers. He meets friends of Lime, some very shady. One of them, Baron Kurtz, claims to have carried the dead man to the side of the street along with another companion, but according to Lime's porter, there was a third man present at the scene of the accident. Martins meets Anna, a friend of Lime, a Czechoslovakian actress hiding in Vienna under false papers. If the Russians – who occupy the ruined city along with the Americans, the British, and the French – discover her, she will be deported. While the chatty porter is assassinated, Major Calloway, from British Military Police, advises Martins to leave Vienna. He informs him that Lime was selling diluted penicillin on the black market which led to a large number of deaths. The American agrees to leave, only for Lime to emerge from the grave. During an encounter on the great Ferris wheel, Wiener Riesenrad, he reveals the extent of his cynicism and amorality, showing an indifference to the fate of his victims, many of whom were children. Shocked, Martins offers to help Calloway trap his friend. In exchange for his assistance, he asks for safe conduct for Anna. Tracked down to the sewers where he is hiding, Harry Lime will meet his end at Martin's bullets, a coup de grace he receives like a favor.

FOUR IN A JEEP

Four in a Jeep is a 1951 Swiss film, co-produced by Leopold Lindtberg (assisted by Elizabeth Montagu – her again). Two years after *The Third Man*, also filmed in the actual locations, it tells of the tribulations of a patrol of four sergeants, an American, a British, a French, and a Russian, who all represent the powers occupying post-war Vienna. The problems start the day they stop a man who has fled a Soviet prison camp. Touched by his story, they decide to help him. But the Russian sergeant's superiors are far from sympathetic. Dilemmas and conflicts escalate in the jeep, perfectly capturing the difficulties of this four-way management of Vienna and the first jolts of a nascent Cold War.

It's exactly the same situation that Graham Greene discovers in his documentary visit in February 1948 to the ancient city of the Habsburgs. A city in ruins, open to all traffic, to all corruptions, divided into four sectors at the hands of the Four Powers and containing one international zone, where crews of four men each representing their respective nation patrol. Cohabitation is difficult, as each of the occupying forces have diverging interests. The Iron Curtain is collapsing, creating an

irreparable partition between the Allies and the Axis forces. For more than forty years, the two blocks would stare daggers at each other, joining in a planetary game of Go, playing according to periods of tension and calm with the near inconceivable prospect of nuclear apocalypse. Four complicated decades that do little to soothe the balance of a world gone bipolar, but favorable for narrative creation. The term "Cold War" – attributed to George Orwell (*Nineteen Eighteen-Four*, *Animal Farm*) who coined it in 1945 – covers the period which only saw an end to hostilities at the fall of the Berlin Wall in 1989 – a prelude to the dissolution of the Soviet Empire. It reached it paroxysm in 1962 with the Cuban Missile Crisis – missiles delivered by the USSR to Fidel Castro's regime and directly threatening the USA. This mano a mano between two superpowers would shape the second half of the twentieth century (and beyond, if one remembers that Vladimir Putin is a product of the KGB) and become the substance of a new golden age of spy literature, in the hands of authors like John Le Carré, Robert Littell, Len Deighton, Ian Fleming, Charles McCarry, and, of course, Graham Greene, whose *The Human Factor* is loosely inspired by the career of his friend Philby. In 1955, the Austrian State Treaty put an end to the partitioning of the country when Moscow made the declaration (1943) that proclaimed the annexing of Austria by the Reich under the name Anschluss null and void. Austria's status as a sovereign state was restored.

Eclipsed by the vast shadow of *The Third Man*, of which it is a kind of natural child, *Four Men in a Jeep* is a fine premonition of the paralyzed world which was looming. A passionate and visionary film, which the first jury of the Berlin International Film Festival awarded a well-deserved Golden Bear and which was later nominated for a Palme D'Or at the 1951 Cannes Film Festival.

BIBLIOGRAPHY

Pourquoi j'écris, Elizabeth Bowen,
V.S. Pritchett, Graham Greene
ÉDITIONS DU SEUIL • 1950

Collected Essays, Graham Greene THE
BODLEY HEAD • 1969

A Sort of Life, Graham Greene
THE BODLEY HEAD • 1971

*The Pleasure Dome: The Collected
Film Criticism 1935-1940*
SECKER & WARBURG • 1972

Ways of Escape, Graham Greene
THE BODLEY HEAD • 1980

The Third Man: Original screenplay,
Graham Greene
FABER AND FABER • 1988

A World of My Own, Graham Greene
REINHARDT BOOKS LTD • 1992

The Graham Greene Film Reader,
edited by David Parkinson
APPLAUSE BOOKS • 1995

*Articles of Faith: The collected Tablet
Journalism of Graham Greene*
SIGNAL BOOKS • 2006

Graham Greene: A Life in Letters,
edited by Richard Greene
LITTLE BROWN • 2007

The Spoken Word,
Graham Greene (audio)
BBC • 2007

Vienna: A poem by Stephen Spender
FABER AND FABER • 1934

*Graham Greene: Témoin des temps
tragiques*, Paul Rostenne
JULLIARD • 1949

Mon ami Graham Greene,
Ronald Matthews
DESCLÉE DE BROUWER • 1957

The Spy's Bedside Book,
Graham Greene, Hugh Greene
RUPERT HART-DAVIS • 1957

Graham Greene, Victor de Pange
(préface by François Mauriac)
ÉDITIONS UNIVERSITAIRES • 1958

OSS, l'Amérique et l'espionnage,
Stewart Alsop, Thomas Bradent
FAYARD • 1964

My Silent War, Kim Philby
(préface by Graham Greene)
MACGIBBON & KEE LTD • 1968

Évangile de Nicodème,
Librairie Droz
GENÈVE • 1973

Graham Greene: L'autre et son double,
interviews with Marie Françoise Allain
BELFOND • 1981

Night and Day, anthology
(préface by Graham Greene)
CHATTO & WINDUS • 1985

*Graham Greene Country,
Visited by Paul Hogarth*
PAVILION BOOKS LTD • 1986

Conversations with Graham Greene,
edited by Henry J. Donaghy
UNIVERSITY PRESS OF MISSISSIPPI • 1992

Graham Greene: The Enemy Within,
Michael Shelden
RANDOM HOUSE • 1994

Greene on Capri: A Memoir,
Shirley Hazzard
VIRAGO PRESS • 2000

The Third Woman, William Cash
LITTLE BROWN AND COMPANY • 2000

Honourable Rebel,
Elizabeth Montagu
MONTAGU VENTURES LTD, 2003

The Life of Graham Greene
(Vol. 1,2,3), Norman Sherry
JONATHAN CAPE • 1989-2004

*In Search of a Beginning:
My Life With Graham Greene*, Yvonne
Cloetta
BLOOMSBURY • 2004

L'agent recruteur, Barbara Honigmann
DENOËL • 2008

*The Defence of The Realm:
the authorized history of MI5*,
Christopher Andrew
ALLEN LANE • 2009

*Philby: Portrait de l'espion en
jeune homme*, Robert Littell
BAKERSTREET • 2011

And of course all the novels by
Graham Greene, with a particular
focus on *The End of the Affair*,
which romantasizes his adventure
with Catherine Walson, and *The
Human Factor*, in which allusions to
the Philby affair abound.